Paul Lichter

SIMON AND SCHUSTER   NEW YORK

We would like to express our appreciation
to the following for their kindness and
cooperation in the production of this book:

Twentieth Century-Fox Film Corporation
Metro-Goldwyn-Mayer
United Artists
Paramount Pictures
Allied Artists
Universal Pictures

and especially to Elvis Presley
for his inspiration.

Copyright © 1975 by Paul Lichter
All rights reserved
including the right of reproduction
in whole or in part in any form
Published by Simon and Schuster
Rockefeller Center, 630 Fifth Avenue
New York, New York 10020

SBN 671-22153-1 Casebound
SBN 671-22154-X Paperback
Library of Congress Catalog Card Number 75-10519
Manufactured in the United States of America

1 2 3 4 5 6 7 8 9 10

DEDICATION

If not for Vernon and Gladys
There wouldn't be Elvis.

If not for Manny and Sylvia
There wouldn't be Paul.

If not for Janice
I wouldn't be me.

And if not for all of these people
This book wouldn't be.

CONTENTS

INTRODUCTION—
THE BOY WHO DARED TO ROCK   10
THE EARLY YEARS   18
    LOVE ME TENDER   24
    LOVING YOU   30
    JAILHOUSE ROCK   36
    KING CREOLE   42
THE GROWING YEARS   48
    G. I. BLUES   52
    FLAMING STAR   56
    WILD IN THE COUNTRY   60
    BLUE HAWAII   64
    FOLLOW THAT DREAM   68
THE LAZY YEARS   72
    KID GALAHAD   76
    GIRLS! GIRLS! GIRLS!   80
    IT HAPPENED AT THE WORLD'S FAIR   84
    FUN IN ACAPULCO   88
    KISSIN' COUSINS   92
    VIVA LAS VEGAS   96
    ROUSTABOUT   102

GIRL HAPPY	106
TICKLE ME	110
HARUM SCARUM	114
PARADISE—HAWAIIAN STYLE	118
FRANKIE AND JOHNNY	122
SPINOUT	126
EASY COME, EASY GO	130
DOUBLE TROUBLE	134
CLAMBAKE	138
STAY AWAY, JOE	142
SPEEDWAY	146
LIVE A LITTLE, LOVE A LITTLE	150
SOMETHING DIFFERENT	154
CHARRO!	156
CHANGE OF HABIT	162
THE TROUBLE WITH GIRLS	166
THE IMAGE	170
THAT'S THE WAY IT IS	172
ELVIS ON TOUR	176
MOVIE MUSIC	183
ABOUT THE AUTHOR	187

SUNDAY - FEB. 6
TWO SHOWS ★ 3:00 p.m. & 8:00 p.m.
AUDITORIUM
MEMPHIS, TENN.

FARON YOUNG
★ "IF YOU AIN'T LOVIN"

MARTHA CARSON
★ BEAUTIFUL GOSPEL SINGER

FERLIN HUSKEY

THE HUSHPUPPIES
Doyle and Teddy
WILBURN BROTHERS

Plus... MEMPHIS' OWN
ELVIS PRESLEY
SCOTTY and BILL
He'll Sing "HEARTBEAKER" - "MILK COW BOOGIE"

MANY MORE...

THE BOY WHO DARED TO ROCK

Where were you in 1954? Are you old enough to remember? Though I hate to admit it, I was ten years old. As a gift for my tenth birthday, my parents gave me a record. It had a yellow and brown label with the word "Sun" across the top. The titles of the two songs were "That's All Right, Mama" and "Blue Moon of Kentucky." The artist, though unknown in 1954, would become the most widely known voice in the history of man. His name—Elvis Presley, The Boy Who Dared To Rock.

One early summer day in 1953, a tall, dark youngster with glossy tousled hair and a strangely engaging mixture of quick friendliness and shyness walked into the office of Sun Record Company in Memphis, Tennessee. It was lunchtime and the president of the company, Sam Phillips, was out. Mrs. Marion Keisker, his receptionist, looked up from her desk and asked, "Can I help you?"

"My name is Elvis Presley and I want to make a record."

No one then, including eighteen-year-old Elvis, would have thought of this moment as having any significance. Yet out of this came one of the most amazing success stories of all time, a rags to riches fable which rivals anything Horatio Alger ever wrote, a true life story which gives affirmation of the American tradition that anyone who can dream and work hard can come from nothing to success.

There are several Elvis Presleys. There is the Elvis who is idolized, the Elvis who is subjected to varying degrees of condemnation, and then there is the legend. There is the man with the searching, brooding eyes and the strangely exciting voice who can stir his audience to an intensity of sexual pleasure which erupts in screams and violent adoration, the giant who sells millions of records and whose presence is box-office magic—who has grossed over one million dollars every year since 1954. There is another man—the friendly, laughing, generous and yet strangely complex Elvis whom his family, friends and associates know.

This is Elvis' story as I got it from following his career from the time his first record, "That's All Right, Mama," began to earn him fame.

The day Elvis walked into Sun Records' office, says Mrs. Keisker, "he was wearing khaki work clothes and was dirty—the dirt was from his job as a truck driver for Crown Electric Company—and he wanted to make a record as a birthday present for his mother. On this day he used his lunch hour to make that record." Mrs. Keisker asked him, "Who do you sing like?" His reply was "I don't sing like anybody but me I reckon." He had no music and was carrying the battered guitar he had made his companion since he was thirteen.

The record he cut that day was called "My Happiness" with "That's When Your Heartaches Begin" on the other side. This record is still in existence, a collector's item if it could be purchased. It cost Elvis four dollars to find out how he sounded. Sam Phillips came back from lunch before the record session (which took all of ten minutes) was completed. When Elvis left, holding his prized record, Phillips commented that Elvis had a sweet voice; though untrained, he was able to do strange things with it.

Several months later he came back and made another record. Sam Phillips listened as Elvis recorded "Casual Love Affair" and "I'll Never Stand in Your Way." (These have never been heard by the public.) Both were sung in an odd mixture of country ballad and pop style. Slow, reedy, with the faint background guitar—but again with the odd lyric sweetness. I believe, however, that few could discern in it what Elvis was to do later. After Elvis left the studio that day, Mrs. Keisker picked up a piece of paper from her desk. It was in Sam Phillips' handwriting and said: "Elvis Presley . . . good ballad singer. Save this." It took the hand of chance to bring Elvis back to the studio again. It was an extraordinary coincidence which played an almost miraculous part in shaping his destiny. Without it, he might still be driving a truck, or working in electrical supply or on a production line.

Phillips, ever on the search for new talent, had brought back from Nashville a demo record of a song called "Without Love (There Is Nothing)." It had been sung by a Negro singer, and they couldn't find out who it was. It was a ballad and Phillips thought it had something. But who would sing it? Mrs. Keisker asked Phillips, "Remember Elvis Presley?" "Yeah," said Sam. "Yes, indeed. Get him on the phone." Mrs. Keisker called Elvis at Crown Electrical Company and asked him to come see them at his convenience. When Mrs. Keisker turned around, there was Elvis. He almost knocked her down coming in. He flashed that famous smile and you would have thought that MGM had just asked him to star in a super movie.

Elvis turned out to be a dismal flop singing "Without Love." It just wasn't his kind of song. But he loved it and many times, after he had become known, Elvis would return to Sun and attempt once again to record it. It wouldn't be until 1969, some fifteen years later, that Elvis would finally record and release "Without Love." Something about Elvis fascinated Phillips, although he didn't know how to catalogue him. Phillips sat Elvis down and made him sing.

"I guess I must have sat there at least three hours," Elvis recalls. "I sang everything I knew . . . pop stuff, spirituals, just a few words of everything I remembered." Phillips got Scotty Moore, a guitarist he knew, and told him to work with Elvis. Then one of the strange coincidences that have figured so often in Elvis' career happened. Scotty lived a few doors from Bill Black, a bull fiddle player. They had knocked around in various hillbilly bands, grubbing for a living the hard way. He thought Bill's bass fiddle would put a little drive behind Elvis. They worked together hour after hour, with Elvis singing all the songs he felt he could do well. "I don't think any of us was too impressed with the other," Bill Black says, his broad face breaking into a grin. "We just happened to like each other. Actually, I think Elvis intended to use my brother on the fiddle if he got a chance to make a record."

The trio assembled in the recording studio and went to work for Sam. Again they went through everything Elvis could remember. Then somehow a song popped into Elvis' head. He tried "That's All Right, Mama." And then, all at once, it was there—the drive, the spontaneous and fantastic vocal effects, the Something. Elvis, Bill and Scotty knew that they had something going, but they didn't know how well until later when they heard the playback.

They backed it up with "Blue Moon of Kentucky," a song Bill Monroe, the famous country singer, had composed and made famous many years before. Sam Phillips was excited. He had his dub and was burning to get it played. He turned over in his mind which disc jockey to try it on; then, on a hunch, he went to WHBQ to see Dewey Phillips, who had been playing rhythm 'n blues for years before the so-called rock 'n roll craze. Dewey played "That's All Right, Mama" on the air, and the plaintive, soaring voice with its odd inflections went out into the night. "That will get them," said Dewey, who had a way of talking that was all his own. "Yessir, that'll get them."

That was in the summer of 1954. Within a week, Sun was struggling with a back order list of some 6,000 records for this unknown new artist, and they didn't have a commercial record pressed. Something tremendous was happening. Sam Phillips realized it. Elvis didn't. He was just hoping. He had been hoping a long time. Sam Phillips then took the record to a country music disc jockey, Sleepy Eye John, who had a big following on WHHM, and he played "Blue Moon of Kentucky." Versions differ on what happened next.

Sleepy Eye himself, who later left for Albuquerque, disclaims any credit for having helped Elvis, but he does have the distinction of having played "Blue Moon" first. Sleepy Eye didn't care for the record and probably wouldn't have played it again, but he left for vacation. The next day, a substitute sitting in for him found the platter and kept it spinning.

Record royalties are paid twice yearly. Here was Elvis with a record that people were buying, and he was like a kid stretching for an ice cream cone held teasingly out of his reach. Elvis was a singer now and he had a record. But how do you go about being a singer, even if you've got a record, with no money and no one to sing to? Rhythm 'n blues disc jockeys refused to play his records because they said Elvis' music was country and western and the country disc jockeys said they were R'nB songs. Elvis began making personal appearances for free, just to get a following. This led to a demand for his records.

A local store owner recalls that one day Elvis was standing in front of his record store and some boys passed by. Elvis' name was becoming known by then and the boys were apparently awed by some of the stories they had heard about the money Elvis had begun to earn. They just barely nodded and looked at him sideways and kept on going. Elvis watched them as they went up the street and then he turned to the owner with tears in his eyes and said, "What's the matter? . . . Those fellows went to school with me and they were my friends, and they didn't even stop to talk."

Bob Neal began to handle Elvis' career in the fall of 1954, shortly after his first record began to be played. Under Bob's direction, Elvis, Scotty and Bill traveled some 25,000 miles. A typical week's schedule ran like this: New Orleans on Friday, Shreveport on Saturday, Memphis Auditorium on Sunday, Ripley, Mississippi, on Monday, Alpine, N.M., on Friday and Saturday. That meant pretty rough traveling for a beat-up Lincoln and sleeping in the car on overnight trips. In late 1954 Sun brought out two new records, "I Don't Care if the Sun Don't Shine" and "Good Rockin' Tonight" plus "Milkcow Blues" and "You're a Heartbreaker." Elvis was hot—the fire started by his personal appearances. He was getting from sixty to seventy-five letters a day from impressed young ladies who had seen him in some wild part of Texas or Arkansas and who ardently desired his picture to keep them company in the lonely months until he next came that way.

At that time Elvis was being billed as "The Hillbilly Cat" and he dressed sharply, with sporty shirts, draped jackets and pegged pants, even though Scotty and Bill wore the traditional semiuniform of cowboy shirt, cowboy belt and tie affected by most country music outfits. His records were still only listed in the C&W charts. Under Bob Neal's leadership, the press was invited to see Elvis perform. A woman reporter for Memphis' largest newspaper had this to say: "I don't know what it is, but he's got it. He moves, he struts, he shakes, he's mean, he's sweet, He's Sex." That headline, along with a three-column picture, ran on the front page of the Memphis paper. His eyes are darkly slumbrous, his hair sleekly long, his sideburns low, and there is a sexy, lazy, tough, good-looking manner which young girls like. It may not be literature, but the description still stands. This story really helped Elvis' career.

His first record was still selling steadily but his other two records were slow getting started. Elvis was being practically ignored by every dee jay except Dewey Phillips, and he wasn't playing Elvis' records often. But the night the article appeared there was an Elvis revival on the air. A lot of people who didn't normally keep up with what went on in country music circuits learned for the first time that they had a genuine phenomenon in their home town. Reprints of the story helped build Elvis as a personality in towns he hadn't played before. Things had been moving fast but now they got faster. Elvis got his first Cadillac, a pink one, and the bookings got bigger. At each show he'd pace back and forth backstage. When he went on stage, it was like someone had turned the electricity on. The celebrated wiggle—and the audience moved. Elvis turned it on hotter and hotter and his followers exploded. The screams and squeals rang in Elvis' ears, and when 1954 came to an end, Elvis had six Cadillacs.

"Before he goes on stage, he'll pace back and forth. But once on stage, it's like a spontaneous eruption of feeling and emotions between performer and audience," says Bob Neal. "Ever since he started, he had been doing a sort of a little bop dance, a rhythmic wiggle with his legs. In 1955, he began to move his left leg in a corkscrew motion. It got a roar from the crowds. Elvis was milking those squeals and screams." Bob Neal was still managing Elvis, but he had problems. He was trying to hold down his own disc jockey job, manage Elvis and keep a wife and five boys happy at home. The last was hard to do because keeping up with Elvis meant being out of town frequently.

"He had gotten so big that it meant I would have to give up everything and go with him," Bob said. "I weighed it. I needed more time with my family." Bob himself helped to arrange the next step in Elvis' career—and a most important step it was. He got together with Colonel Tom Parker and they came to terms. Colonel Parker was one of the country's most colorful behind-the-scenes personalities, a shrewd businessman with contacts from coast to coast. He had the know-how to get Elvis something besides the regional recognition which had been his.

On November 22, 1955, this story appeared in the Memphis *Press-Scimitar:* "Elvis Presley, 20, Memphis recording star and entertainer who zoomed into big-time and big money almost overnight, has been released from his contract with Sun Record Co. of Memphis and will record exclusively for RCA Victor."

Both Sam Phillips and RCA officials said at the time that the money involved was believed to be the highest ever paid for a contract release for a country and western artist, which was how Elvis was still being considered. What made it more unusual was that Elvis, still only twenty, had only one more year to go on his contract with Sun. *Billboard* reported that the price was "a reported payoff of $40,000." With the contract, RCA got the rights to the five released Sun songs. Involved in the deal besides Colonel Parker, Bob Neal and Phillips was Coleman Tiley 3rd of RCA. Colonel Parker also arranged for establishing Elvis Presley Music, a publishing firm, in conjunction with Hill and Range Music, Inc. of New York. There was a great deal of snickering in some record industry circles at the deal. This was really taking a chance. But Colonel Parker, RCA Victor and Elvis had the last laugh. Parker had made stars of Eddy Arnold and Hank Snow, whom he still managed at the time. He knew every trick of the trade, and things began to happen fast.

Colonel Parker landed Elvis a five-time deal on the "Jackie Gleason Presents the Dorsey Brothers" TV show. CBS began giving Elvis a build-up as Tommy Dorsey's discovery. Dorothy Kilgallen's column carried an item on Dorsey's "discovery." Both *Billboard* and *Cash Box* named Elvis "most promising new singer in the country and western field for the year." Elvis got up on the Dorsey show and poured it on. The first week he got a big hand. By his second week things were really hot, with a full brigade of bobby soxers squealing and screaming in ecstasy, trying to get to this new idol when he came off stage.

The doorman at CBS TV's New York studio was quoted as saying, "I have never seen anything like it." It was during this period that Elvis' popularity shifted significantly. Elvis was no longer a country star, he was also a rhythm and blues star and a pop star. He introduced "Heartbreak Hotel" and "I Was the One" on the Dorsey show. Strangely, it was "I Was the One" that overnight became number one on the Memphis radio stations. It was much later that "Heartbreak Hotel" took over the number one rating in Memphis. One of the New York papers had this to say about Elvis' Dorsey show appearances: "Presley puts intensity into his songs. Overemotional? Yes. But he projects. He sells!" Elvis had definitely arrived. You can't throw that much into something without its telling. "Heartbreak Hotel" was selling like wildfire and so was everything else Elvis recorded. His first album was released and it went right to the top of *Billboard*'s chart.

From the beginning of his national exposure on TV, Elvis became controversial. The network received thousands of letters from viewers who thought Elvis' dancing was "vulgar" and "obscene." The storm continued to rage and intensified after Elvis' first appearance on the Milton Berle Show. Two turnaway audiences of over five thousand people paid $15,000 to hear him sing eight songs in the San Diego Arena. The arena manager had to call out the police and a platoon of Shore Patrol to handle the mob who pursued Elvis to his dressing room. In El Paso he was mauled pretty badly. They had already started trying to get at him at close quarters and he considered himself lucky to have a shirt on his back. "One girl took a swipe at me and really clawed my side," he said. "It stung pretty bad for a while."

Although he was already on his way to becoming a legend, Elvis' rise had been so rapid that some people hadn't caught up with it. In some midwestern schools, one of those recurrent rumors cropped up that he was dead and the students evidently were so upset that they weren't going to school. A newspaper called Paramount to check the report that Elvis had died and a studio publicity man said, "Who in the hell is Elvis Presley?" In June, the AP out of New York called Elvis' office to find out if the stories of his death were true. Elvis answered the phone and thought the question over, sat for a moment, then burst out laughing. "If some people had their way maybe I would be," he said. Still later in June, United Press queried on a report that Elvis had been secretly married for two weeks to the daughter of a nationally prominent financier and industrialist. It seemed absurd, but those things have to be checked out. Just two nights before, Elvis had been happily dating an old Memphis girlfriend, but now he had left on tour. A long distance phone call to Colonel Parker in New York brought a chuckle from him. "He hasn't got hitched unless he did it in the last hour or so." Further checking revealed that the financier mentioned had three daughters, all happily married. Another frequent rumor was that Elvis was on dope. "I don't smoke and I've never had an alcoholic drink," he said, "and furthermore, I don't ever intend to."

The following is one way that such a rumor gets started: A New York columnist carried an item about an unidentified "rock 'n roll king" who was, this columnist told us authoritatively, being watched by two detectives because his manager was afraid that his orgies with weed and women would erupt in scandal. A few days later, in the same column, there was an item to the effect that "Elvis Presley has to have guards on stage with him at every appearance." Some reasoned it was the same person. One heartbroken youngster wrote that this couldn't be anyone but Elvis because he was the undisputed Rock 'N Roll King. She said that he would have her undying devotion all her days, dope fiend or not.

But criticism was nothing new to Elvis. He had been kidded as a boy about his sideburns but he had stubbornly kept them. There are contradictory impulses in Elvis. He longs for respect and response, but the most positive affirmation of this to him is in the screams of his audience—so here goes that writhing movement again. "The trouble is," said one of Elvis' friends, "that he doesn't think he's going over unless they're tearing the house down and he'll just keep working on them until he has them where he wants them." The critics measured Elvis by their own backgrounds and by what they expected of music, rather than for what he is, what he has accomplished and what his music represents.

Elvis, with his broken syllables and strange vocal effects, uses his voice like the guitar he has carried since he was a boy. If the critics had regarded it as what it was, an uncultivated but genuine music on the level with folk music, and if they had listened to it without preconceived prejudices, they might have come to some different conclusions. But Elvis took a beating in print. How did it affect him? "I don't like it, but I have to expect it, I guess," he said. He shrugs it off . . . but he has every unkind, bitter, cruel word he has ever come across about himself in a scrap book. His mother and father keep it for him. Seldom has there been such a wholesale defiance of the power of the press. The press criticized, and Elvis was becoming the number one attraction in the country—on stage, records and television.

In the history of show business, there has never been anyone quite like Elvis Aron Presley. And never has a performer been so controversial.

Elvis appeared on the Steve Allen Show. He wore tails, didn't move and sang "I Want You, I Need You, I Love You." He was involved in a comedy skit along with Allen, Imogene Coca and Andy Griffith; he sang a few lines about "Tonto Candy Bars." He also introduced "Hound Dog," which he sang to a basset hound. It was Steve Allen's idea to have Elvis dress in formal attire and to tone him down.

Ed Sullivan stole Elvis away, signing him for three historic appearances for the then record-breaking sum of $50,000. Elvis' first appearance on the Sullivan show evoked more protests. Elvis sang "Hound Dog" and "Don't Be Cruel" and "Reddy Teddy." Critics had this to say about his classic performance: "He injected movements of the tongue and indulged in wordless singing that was singularly distasteful." "In some ways it was perhaps the most unpleasant thing I've ever seen." The teenagers did not find it unpleasant. The girls especially found Elvis and his revolving pelvis immensely heartening. "We love Elvis," crowds chanted outside the stage door. And Elvis loved them right back. He repeated his September 9th triumph when, on October 28th, he returned to the Sullivan show. This time he introduced the song "Love Me," which made recording history as it became the only song that was never released as a single to reach the singles charts. "Love Me" was on the second Elvis LP and was released on the 45 extended play No. 992. This feat has never been duplicated. On November 19, 1956, *Love Me Tender* opened at New York's Paramount Theater. The crowd waiting to get in numbered in the thousands. Critics from coast to coast slammed Elvis' acting ability. Nevertheless, the film established Elvis as a major Hollywood star.

Elvis' private life was just as hectic. On October 18th, Elvis got into a fight with two service station attendants. The fisticuffs flared when Ed Hopper became irate because a crowd drawn by Elvis and his $10,000 car was blocking business at the gas pumps. Hopper slapped Elvis on the back of his head and told him to move on. Elvis jumped out of the car and crossed a right that set Hopper on his heels. Another attendant, Aubrey Brown, 6'4" tall and 220 pounds, moved in and also drew a right. Elvis appeared in Memphis City Court along with the two men he had outfought. Presley was cleared, but his two opponents were fined on assault and battery charges.

In Chicago, at the International Amphitheater, thirteen thousand showed up to see Elvis. Elvis showed up also, wearing a suit made of gold lamé. This was the first time Elvis was seen wearing his now-legendary jumpsuit of gold. By the time the year 1956 drew to an end, "Heartbreak Hotel," "I Was the One," "I Want You, I Need You, I Love You," "Don't Be Cruel," "Hound Dog," and "Love Me Tender" had all sold over one million copies each and Elvis Presley was a movie star.

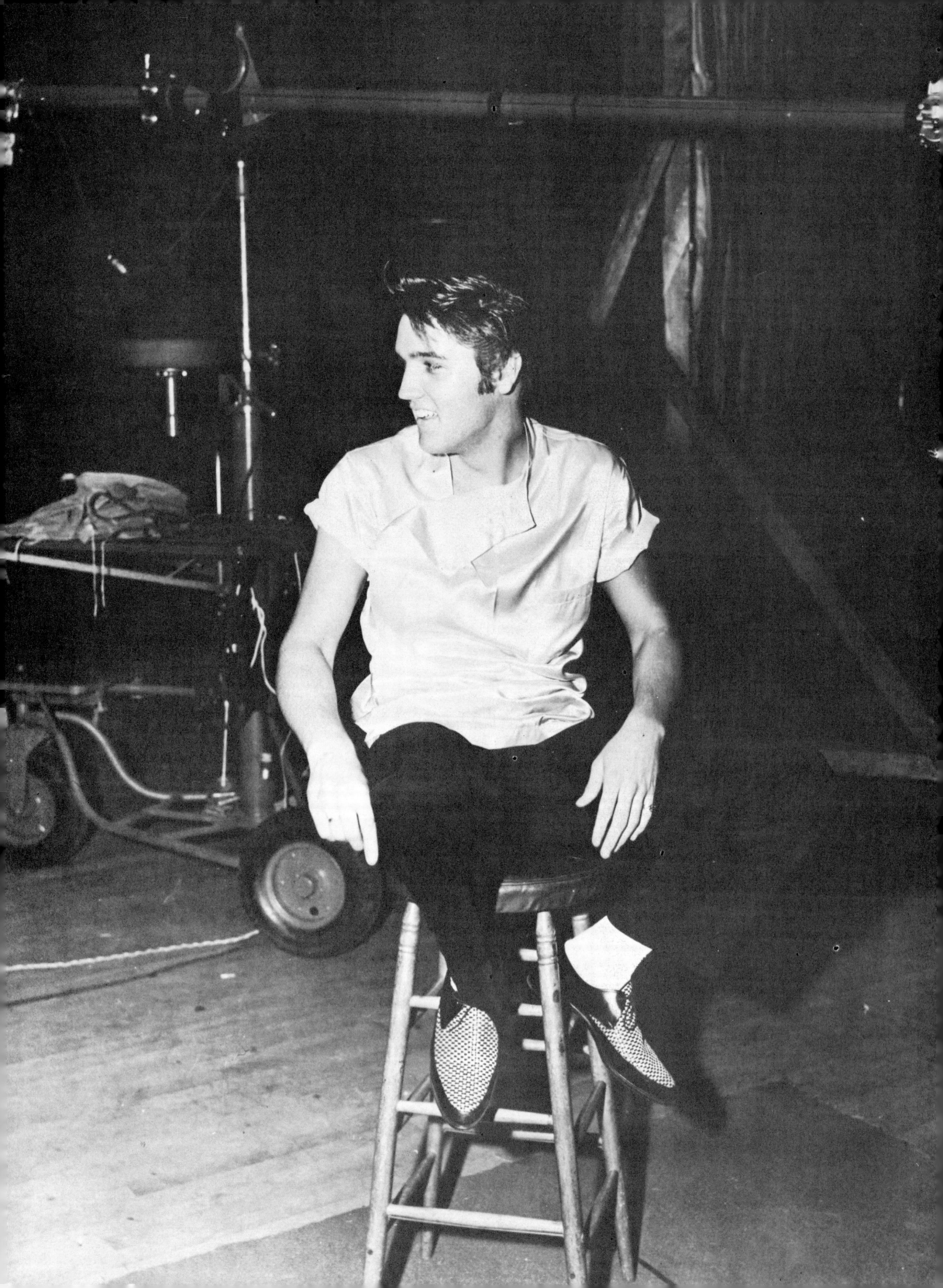

THE EARLY YEARS

Elvis' ambition all his life had been to be a movie actor. "A good one," he emphasized. *Love Me Tender,* his first film, was a Civil War picture. Elvis costarred with Richard Egan and Debra Paget. Although he sang in *Love Me Tender,* Elvis took the part primarily for its dramatic appeal. And what qualifications did he have as an actor? Abe Lastfogel, then the head of the William Morris Agency, told his friends, "His screen test was one of the best I ever saw."

Elvis was not only handsome, but he had a mobile, expressive face, able to mirror gaiety or tenderness, and sometimes an inscrutable brooding quality. A man at Twentieth Century-Fox watched Elvis on the set of *Love Me Tender* and said in some wonder, "The boy never had an acting lesson in his life, but there's a natural quality about his acting. He acts the way he sings."

Hollywood was a new experience for Elvis. He had been a night person, accustomed to going to bed at dawn. In Hollywood they got him up at 5:30 in the morning so he would get to the studio in time for makeup. When asked if the absence of a live audience bothered him, he answered, "No. I figured I was playing to an audience in the long run, anyway."

Elvis was happy in Hollywood except for one thing—it kept him away from home so long. Often he chartered special planes just to give him a few hours with his mother and father and friends. For ten weeks Elvis was in Hollywood working on his second picture, *Loving You.* He worked hard and he played a little, but mostly he worked. While filming *Loving You,* he dated Rita Moreno several times and also saw Yvonne Lime. "Yvonne is fun to be with," he said.

Elvis signed with MGM to make his third film. In *Jailhouse Rock* Elvis was to play a tough guy from the wrong side of the tracks who gets in trouble with the law. He goes to jail, meets an older man, also a prisoner, who recognizes the young man's musical talent. When they get out, the older man manages Elvis' career.

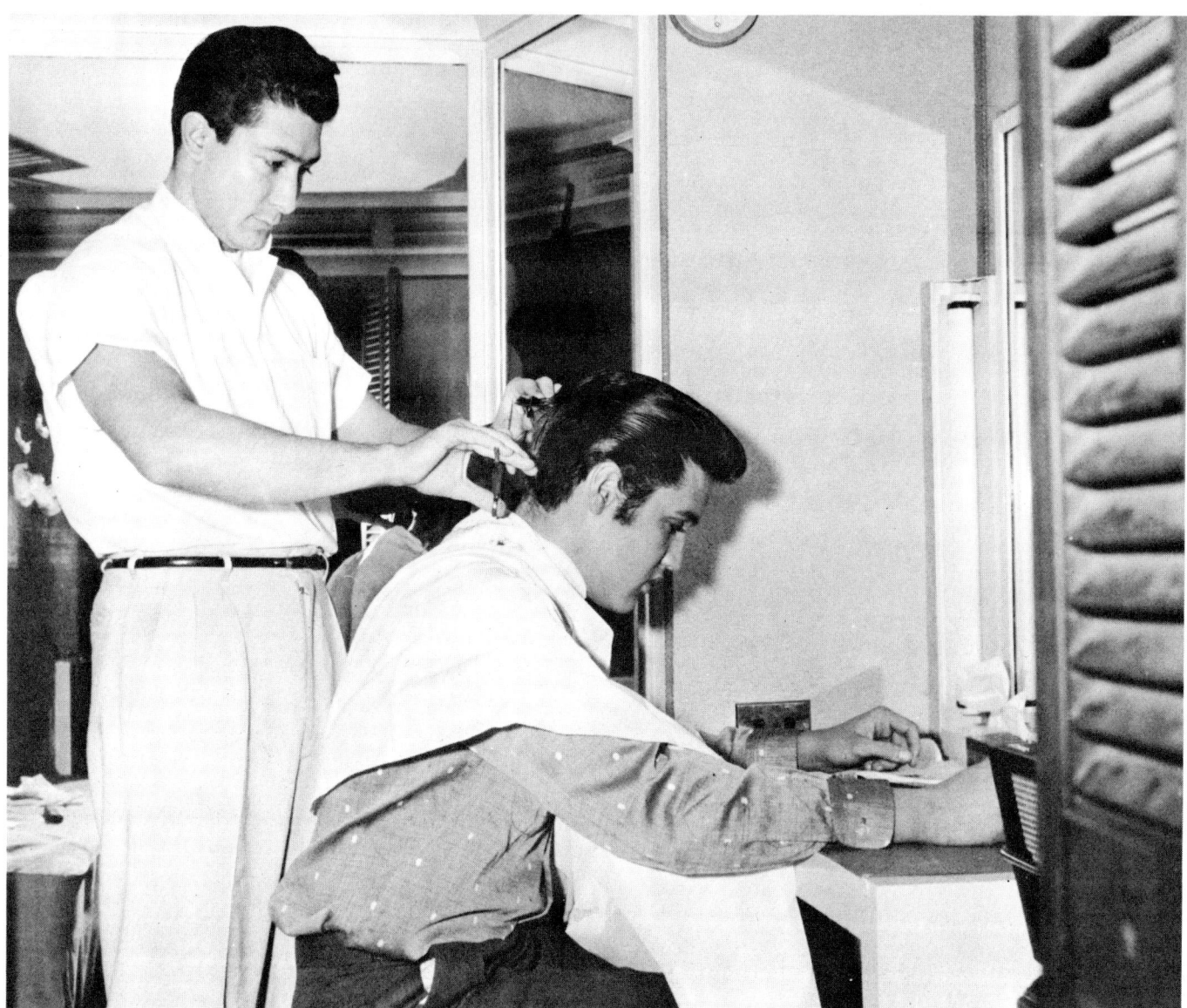

Hal Wallis, who produced *Loving You* for Paramount, was able to catch Elvis' early stage act on film better than anyone has to date. There were a lot of stories around Hollywood at the time saying that Elvis would copy or imitate the late James Dean. Elvis had this to say: "I don't want to copy anyone. I was a powerful admirer of James Dean. I think he was one of the greatest actors I've ever seen. He and Marlon Brando and a whole bunch more I could call. But I'm not going to try and copy anybody. I'm trying to be myself in my acting, with my own name and my own style of acting." After completing the excellent *Jailhouse Rock,* Elvis signed with Paramount to star in *King Creole.* The film was based on Harold Robbins' *A Stone for Danny Fisher,* and was directed by Michael Curtiz, the mastermind of *Casablanca.*

During the filming of *King Creole* Elvis was drafted by the United States Army and, for a while, it looked as though he wouldn't be able to complete the film. But, with Paramount's help, Elvis managed to have his induction delayed long enough to enable him to complete his fourth motion picture. In *King Creole* Elvis starred with a first-rate cast, including Carolyn Jones, Dolores Hart, Walter Matthau, Dean Jagger and Vic Morrow.

In this, his fourth film, Elvis really came of age. He gave his fans and the critics something to remember him by while he served his country. It would be a little over two years before Elvis would return to Hollywood. *King Creole* left the critics shouting "Oscar" for Elvis, and to his fans Elvis had given a performance he would never duplicate.

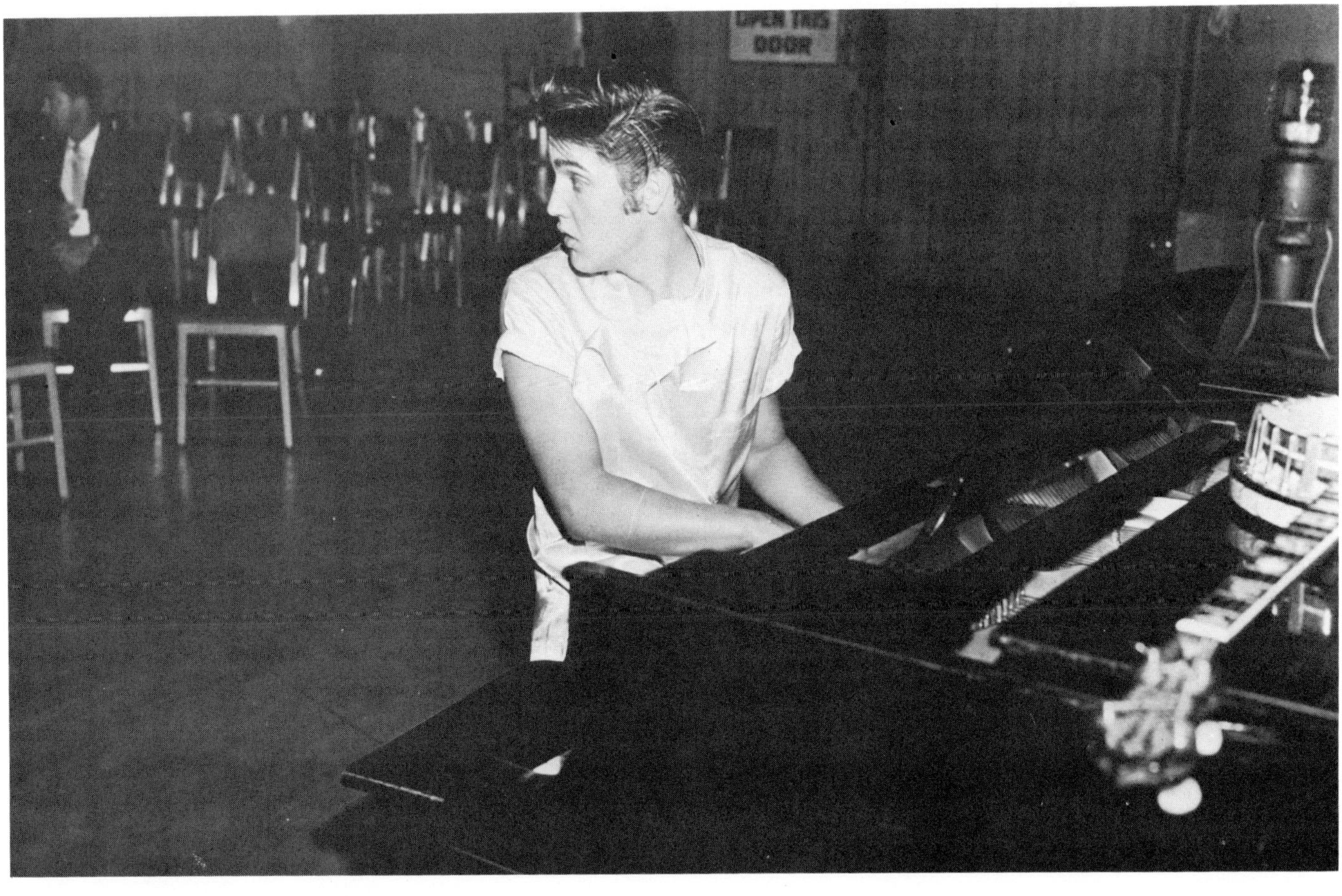

23

A Twentieth Century-Fox Picture (1956)

Cast

Richard Egan, Debra Paget, Elvis Presley, Robert Middleton, William Campbell, Neville Brand, Mildred Dunnock, Bruce Bennett, James Drury, Russ Conway, Ken Clark, Barry Coe, L. Q. Jones, Paul Burns, Jerry Sheldon

Credits

Produced by David Weisbart. Directed by Robert D. Webb. Screenplay by Robert Buckner. Based on a story by Maurice Geraghty. Music by Lionel Newman.

Synopsis

Lt. Vance Reno (Richard Egan), his two younger brothers—Brett (William Campbell) and Ray (James Drury)—his sergeant, Mike Gavin (Neville Brand), and troopers Davis (Barry Coe), Fleming (L. Q. Jones) and Kelso (Ken Clark), members of a Confederate cavalry troop, rob a Federal Army payroll in the last days of the Civil War. When they learn the war is over they divide the money and head home.

The family reunion is marred, however, when Vance learns that his kid brother, Clint (Elvis Presley), has married Vance's former sweetheart, Cathy (Debra Paget), after hearing that Vance had been killed. Realizing the situation is his own personal tragedy, Vance decides to leave and plans to say his farewell to Cathy at a family picnic at which Clint entertains with some songs.

U.S. Army Major Kincaid (Bruce Bennett) and Pinkerton detective Siringo (Robert Middleton) arrive to arrest the Reno brothers. Although they deny their guilt, they are taken to trial. But Clint plots with Gavin, Kelso and Fleming to rescue his brothers. Just as Vance agrees to return the money, Gavin makes a raid and frees the Reno boys, who now become fugitives.

When Gavin and the others refuse to give up the money, Vance disarms them and takes their share, intending to exchange the money for their freedom. But at the farm, he finds a posse waiting for them. Cathy hides the money in her dress and meets Vance in a nearby cabin. There he tells her that he will leave as soon as he has cleared himself, but she asks him to stay. Meanwhile the enraged Gavin turns Clint against Vance by saying that Vance ran away with both Cathy and the money. Vance, however, has returned to town to give up the money and is returning to the cabin so that he and Cathy can explain their feelings to Clint. On his arrival, he sees Cathy and Gavin's men there ahead of him. As Vance climbs the hill to the cabin, Gavin hands Clint a gun and tells him to shoot. He does and wounds Vance. Realizing what he has done, he rushes to Vance's side, pleading for understanding. Gavin moves in to finish off the wounded Vance, but Clint, defending him, is mortally wounded. As he dies, Clint whispers that everything is all right now for everyone.

Meanwhile, Siringo has the money and the war between the Federals and the Renos is over at last. Later, at the farmhouse, Mrs. Reno (Mildred Dunnock) and Cathy look at each other and in the mother's eyes is the knowledge that time, along with Vance's love, is a great healer.

with Richard Egan and Debra Paget

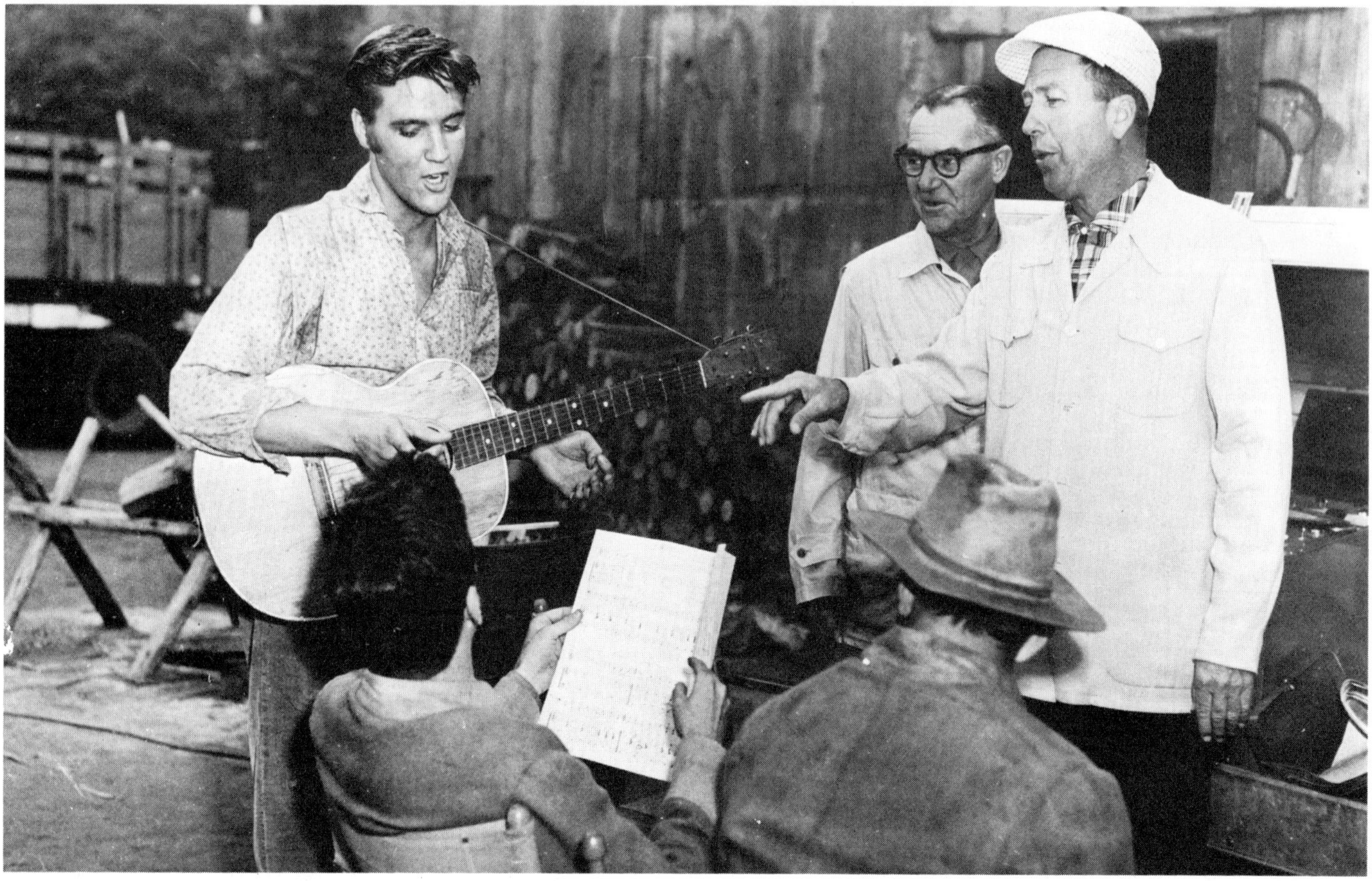

with Debra Paget

His first film, *Love Me Tender,* gave us a blond Elvis performing great songs that fit into the film very well. Richard Egan and Debra Paget, two of the screen's top acting talents, were Elvis' costars. In this, his first exposure in movies, Elvis more than held his own.

A Paramount Picture (1957)

Cast

Elvis Presley, Lizabeth Scott, Wendell Corey, Dolores Hart, James Gleason, Ralph Dumke, Paul Smith, Ken Becker, Jana Lund

Credits

Produced by Hal B. Wallis. Directed by Hal Kanter. Screenplay by Herbert Baker and Hal Kanter. From a story by Mary Agnes Thompson.

Synopsis

Deke Rivers (Elvis Presley), a young truck driver, wows the crowd at a political rally where he has come to deliver beer but remains to sing a hot number with the band, at the urging of glamorous press agent Glenda Markle (Lizabeth Scott). Glenda and Tex Warner (Wendell Corey), the leader of the band, offer Deke a singing job, although they have a girl singer, Susan Jessup (Dolores Hart).

The band makes a round of small town appearances, with Deke's popularity increased by every stopover. Glenda gets him to sign a personal contract for her to represent him, without letting Tex know. Though he is deeply interested in Susan, Deke becomes attracted to Glenda, whose publicity gimmicks soon make him a celebrity. His buildup leads to a booking in a big theater where he learns what it means to be a celebrity. Teenagers mob his car and demand autographs. The theater does standing-room-only business. Carl (James Gleason), Glenda and Tex' booking agent, plans a one-man concert for Deke in a Dallas suburb, and for a big, splashy publicity stunt, Glenda and Tex buy him a red and white convertible, pretending that it's an anonymous gift from an oil-rich widow. To pay for the car they have to cut expenses. Susan is among those fired. To console her, Deke drives Susan to her farm home. The two have a great time together, only to be followed by Glenda, who is furious and brings Deke back to town.

The car stunt arouses antagonism toward Deke. Unhappy, Deke wants to leave and go to Susan's farm. Glenda dissuades him, their conversation ending in an embrace. While Deke is rehearsing for a big telecast Glenda has set up for him, he learns from Tex that Glenda is Tex' former wife and that Tex hopes they'll get together again. Miserable, Deke leaves town in his old jalopy and has a smashup. Glenda finds him unhurt, physically. She tells him the truth about the publicity stunt and frees him from his contract. He does the telecast.

With Susan beside him, Deke accepts a big TV contract and asks Tex and Glenda, who now plan to remarry, to represent him.

with Jana Lund

Loving You was Elvis' second film and the first to show him with black hair. The film was also the first and only color Elvis film until almost four years later, when he returned from the army to make *G. I. Blues*. *Loving You* captured Elvis' early stage act better than it has ever been caught in any other film. The soundtrack was possibly the best of any Elvis film, with every song a standout. Outstanding songs included: "Lonesome Cowboy," "Loverdoll," "Teddy Bear," "Mean Woman Blues" and "Loving You."

with Dolores Hart

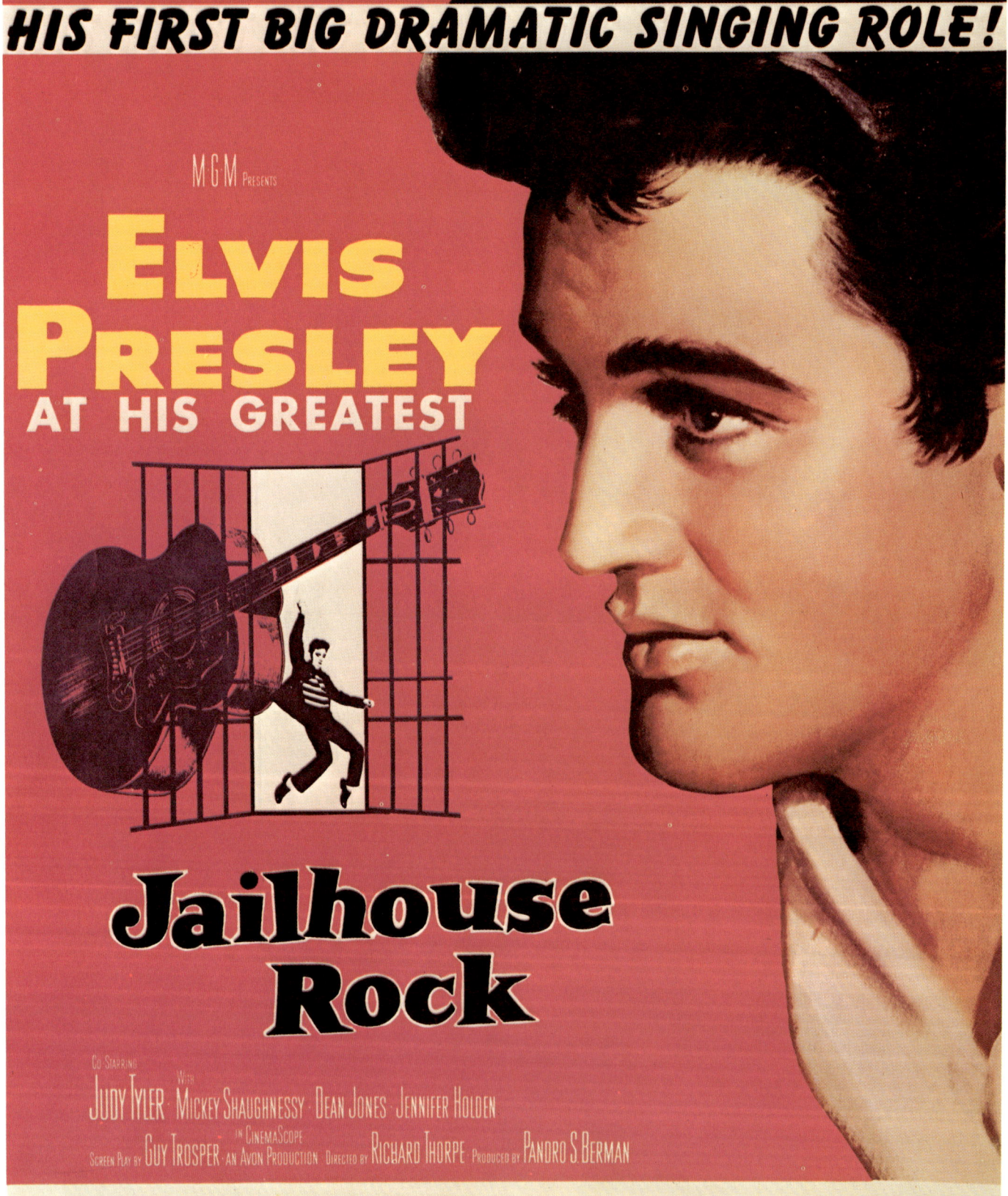

A Metro-Goldwyn-Mayer Picture (1957)

Cast

Elvis Presley, Judy Tyler, Mickey Shaughnessy, Vaughan Taylor, Jennifer Holden, Dean Jones, Ann Neyland

Credits

Produced by Pandro S. Berman. Directed by Richard Thorpe.
Screenplay by Guy Trosper.

Synopsis

Vince (Elvis Presley) is an ordinary truck driver who stops in for a drink at a nightclub where he is pestered by a woman. One of the men at the bar objects to Vince's having anything to do with this woman and starts a fight. During the scuffle, Vince accidentally knocks the man's head against the wall and he dies. Vince is sentenced to prison for manslaughter.

His prison cellmate is Hunk Houghton (Mickey Shaughnessy), a former western cowboy singer. At first he is unsociable to Vince, but as the days pass he allows Vince to play a few chords on his guitar and then lets him sing, accompanying himself on the guitar.

A few months later the prison gives a television special in which the prisoners take part. Vince is one of the acts, the act that receives more attention than all the others put together. Sacks of fan mail arrive for Vince. Hunk persuades the post office department of the prison to keep the fan mail a secret; therefore Vince never gets to know about it. Hunk then draws up a contract, which he asks Vince to sign. The contract states that when they leave prison they will become a team act and share the profits equally. Feeling he has nothing to lose, Vince signs.

One day in the prison dining room, one of Vince's friends complains about the food and throws his meal across the room. A fight ensues and Vince is blamed for starting it. He is whipped as punishment.

Eventually the day comes when Vince is to be released and it is only then that he is told about the huge amount of mail his one appearance earned him. He finds himself a room to live in and attempts to sort through all the letters.

The next place he visits is a nightclub where he begins to talk to Peggy Van Alden (Judy Tyler), an exploitation girl for a famous record company. Determined to become a singer, Vince jumps up on the stage after the act finishes and starts to sing. No one is interested and one man starts to laugh. Although he is not particularly laughing at Vince, Vince leaps off the stage and knocks him out!

Peggy is interested though, and she persuades him to make a tape. On hearing the tape, even Vince agrees that, if he wants to become a star, he has got to try a different style of singing. He tries again, this time throwing everything he has into it and the result pleases everyone. Peggy goes with Vince to try to persuade a recording executive to buy the tape and record it. At first the executive refuses but then accepts mysteriously. The record is released and Peggy and Vince rush to the nearest record store and listen to the disc in one of the listening booths. The record turns out to be a different version—by one of the contract artists of the recording executive. Vince's song belongs to an established recording artist. Seething with anger, Vince lets the executive know just how he feels . . . with one of his famous right crosses.

Peggy and Vince decide that the only thing to do is to start a company of their own. They do everything themselves, including the wholesaling and distribution. It has become apparent to everyone but Vince that Peggy is in love with him. Her emotions reach a climax when she asks Vince one evening in his room if there is anything else besides money that interests him. He answers, "What else is there?" Peggy arranges a party so that she can take Vince home to meet her parents. Vince doesn't like the attitude of the other guests and he walks out. Peggy runs after him but cannot persuade him to return.

Peggy doesn't see much of Vince after that and it appears that he has forgotten her. His main romantic interest seems to be Shelley Wilson (Jennifer Holden), who is to play the part of his leading lady in a film. By this time Hunk has been let out of prison and Vince has been forced, because of their old contract, to find him a spot on his television special. The director of the show, however, refuses to let Hunk appear and Vince keeps him on as his personal assistant—receiving one tenth of all the profits.

One night, Hunk comes in determined to start a fight with Vince. Vince won't argue with him and Hunk delivers a deadly punch to his throat. Vince will have to undergo surgery with no certainty that he will ever sing again. "Test Day" arrives with Vince afraid to try out his voice. After much persuasion, Vince agrees to sing with only his pianist present. Everyone leaves the room until they hear those same mellow tones. Everything ends on a happy note with Vince singing "Young and Beautiful" to Peggy.

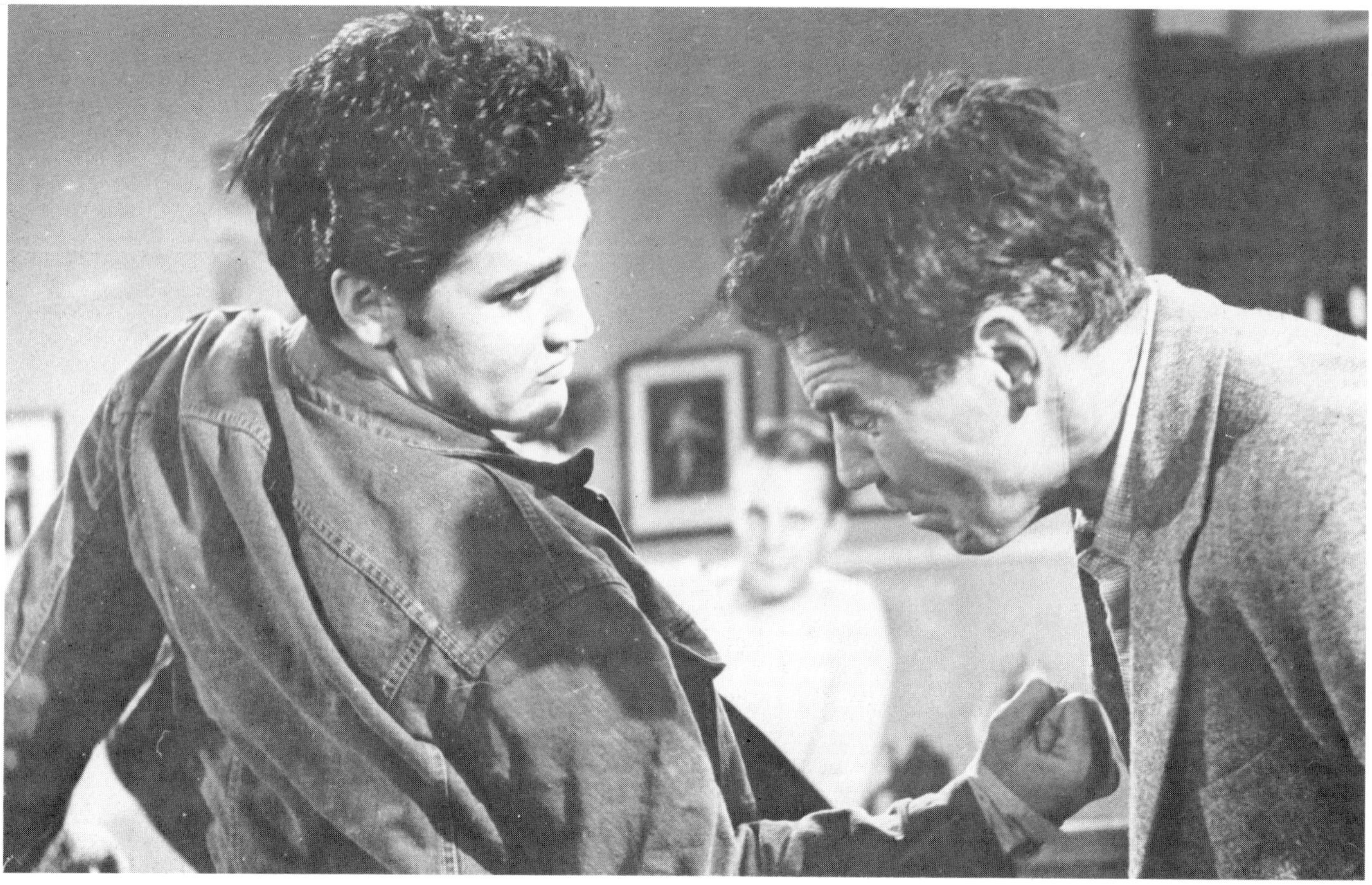

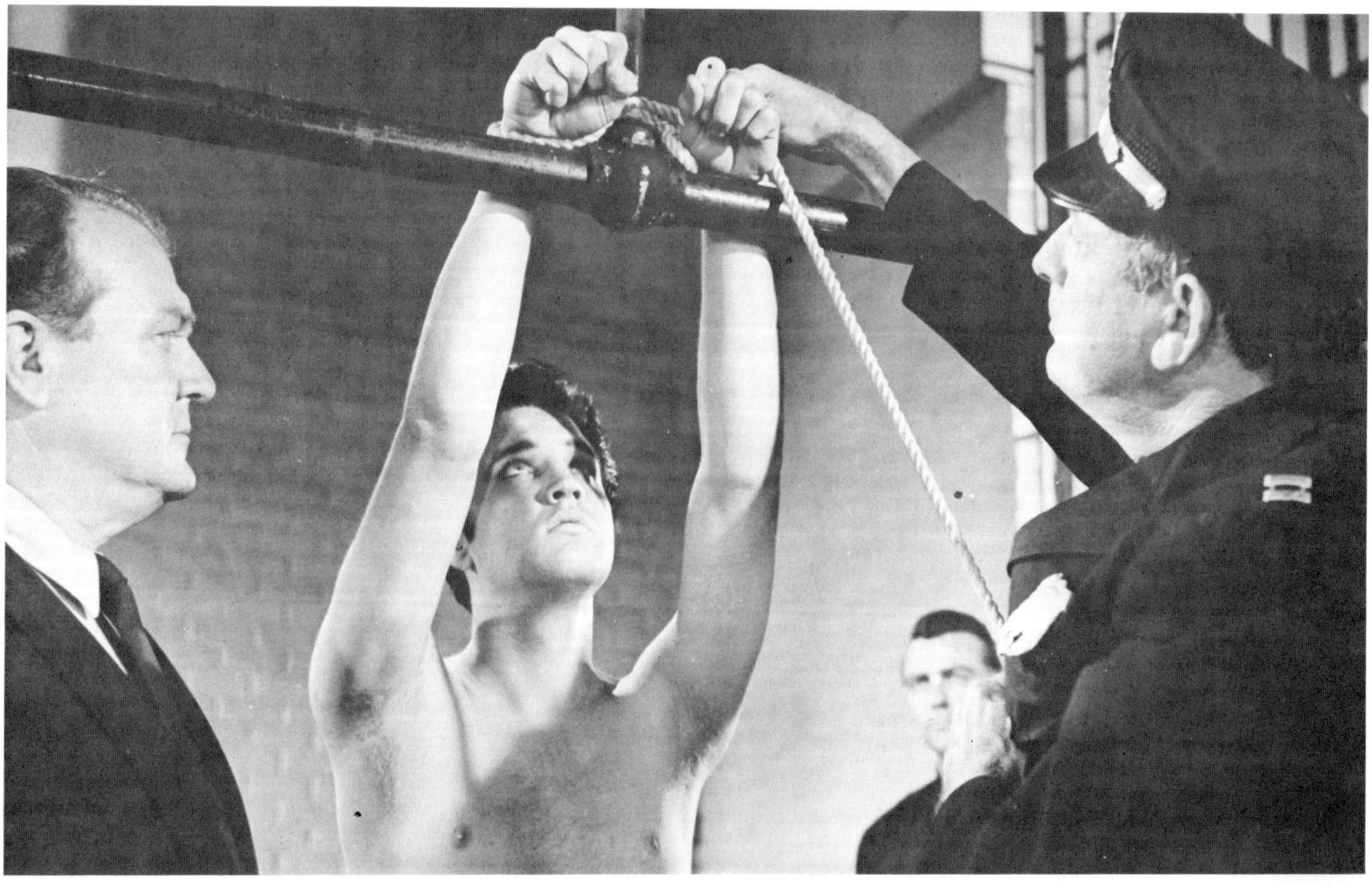

with Judy Tyler

with Judy Tyler

Jailhouse Rock had the critics calling Elvis a singing James Dean. He was cast as an angry young man much like his own public image in the fifties. Great soundtrack with "Treat Me Nice" and "Young and Beautiful" as standout songs. The standout scene and probably the best musical production number of Elvis' career is the title number, "Jailhouse Rock." The film showed an accurate view of an ambitious young man and his bouts with the world on both sides of the prison bars.

A Paramount Picture (1958)

Cast

Elvis Presley, Carolyn Jones, Dolores Hart, Dean Jagger, Liliane Montevecchi, Walter Matthau, Jan Shepard, Paul Stewart, Vic Morrow

Credits

Produced by Hal B. Wallis. Directed by Michael Curtiz. Associate Producer—Paul Nathan. Screenplay by Herbert Baker and Michael Vincente Gazzo. Based upon the novel "A Stone for Danny Fisher" by Harold Robbins.

Synopsis

Early in the morning of his last day of high school, Danny Fisher (Elvis Presley) goes to clean up the Blue Shade, a cheap nightspot on Bourbon Street in New Orleans' French Quarter, where he works as a busboy because his father (Dean Jagger) can't hold a job. There an all-night drinking party is still in progress and, after being forced to sing a song, he rescues Ronnie (Carolyn Jones) from a pawing hoodlum. Ronnie, property of racketeer Maxie Fields (Walter Matthau), wants to break away from him but doesn't dare.

Late for school, Danny gets into a fight with classmates who see Ronnie kiss him goodbye and is told by the principal that he will not graduate. In an alley outside, he is jumped by three young hoods led by Shark (Vic Morrow), whose brother was beaten by Danny. Despite the odds, Danny wins both the fight and the grudging admiration of the three, who ask him to join them. Danny turns them down.

Back home, Danny's father announces that he has a new job in a drugstore and asks Danny to return to school full time. Instead, Danny joins Shark and his friends, acting as a decoy by singing while they rob a five-and-dime store. Before leaving, Danny sits at the soda fountain and is waited on by Nellie (Dolores Hart), with whom he makes a date. That night Danny is working at the Blue Shade when Ronnie walks in with Maxie. Danny greets her but, to allay Maxie's suspicions, she pretends she doesn't know him, that she only heard him sing once. Maxie challenges Danny to prove he can sing, which he does; he is promptly offered a singing job at the King Creole, a dying nightclub owned by Charlie LeGrand (Paul Stewart), the only man on Bourbon Street independent of Maxie.

Danny defies his father, accepts Charlie's offer, is a big hit and packs the King Creole nightly. Though he dates the marriage-minded Nellie, he and Ronnie have a strong pull to each other, but she fears Maxie too much to give in to it. Maxie brazenly uses her to get Danny to quit the King Creole and go to work for him, but Ronnie begs Danny not to get involved with Maxie the way she did. When Danny refuses Maxie, the racketeer calls in Shark and orders him to get something big on him. The "something big" involves a holdup implicating Danny and landing his father in the hospital.

In a rage, Danny gives Maxie a terrible beating, setting every hoodlum in town after him. After a showdown with Shark, Danny, in bad shape, is taken by Ronnie to her country hideout and nursed to health. Maxie tracks them down, kills Ronnie and is himself killed by one of his own men whom Danny had befriended. Danny returns to the King Creole, to Nellie and his family.

with Walter Matthau and Vic Morrow

with Vic Morrow

with Carolyn Jones

King Creole was the best thing that ever happened to Elvis because it caused the critics to admit that he was a great actor. The film featured what I consider, along with "Loving You," the best soundtrack of any Elvis film. Every kind of song was used to its best advantage. There were tender ballads, blues, great rock numbers and dixieland. There was enough to satisfy any fan—enough, in fact, to satisfy any member of the family, even though some of the fight scenes were rather savage and realistic. The script was one of the best—based on *A Stone for Danny Fisher*—and Elvis obviously had a great time portraying the lusty Danny.

THE GROWING YEARS

America's favorite singing soldier came home to his fans and his home. His service hitch was over, but Elvis, when he got home in 1960, had a screen extension—he was drafted to star in Paramount's *G.I. Blues,* which audiences could identify with Elvis' own experience. On the set, Elvis particularly enjoyed the little differences between the movie version of life in the service and his real memories. He'd been away for two years and it was a great feeling to be welcomed back by the millions of Presley fans. In the film, Elvis starred with Juliet Prowse, forming a combination that worked so well it made the move from the set to his personal life.

Once Elvis got into the swing of moviemaking again, he announced that he would like to play all types of roles. Twentieth Century-Fox chose Elvis to star in *Flaming Star,* in a role that was written for Marlon Brando. *Flaming Star* was a western and, although it was a good one, the box office suffered because fans were not prepared to see Elvis in a dramatic role.

Women had always gone wild at Presley movies—wives and mothers, as well as teenagers. *Flaming Star,* in large part, was a man's picture and gave the whole family something to enjoy.

Elvis had established a heavy schedule for himself—two movies a year, records and special projects. He began his 1961 screen chores with *Wild In The Country,* a Twentieth Century-Fox movie with a Peyton Place feeling to it. Once again Elvis' acting was praised but the film was slow at the box-office. His second film in 1961 would be a musical. In Paramount's *Blue Hawaii,* Elvis played a native against a background of lush scenery and beautiful girls, with a cast featuring Joan Blackman and Angela Lansbury. The film had fourteen songs in it, and, of all his many movies, *Blue Hawaii* was by far his most successful. The soundtrack recording sold over six million dollars' worth of LPs.

Other stars, following the success of *Blue Hawaii,* tried to imitate Elvis' beach format, but credit for the first such movie has to go to Elvis. His next film was United Artists' *Follow That Dream,* a delightful comedy which showed us a different Elvis. A critic had this to say about Elvis' performance: "Whatever it is . . . the boy's got it."

on the set of *Flaming Star*

with Mark King, Executive Assistant to Mayor Henry Loeb, Memphis

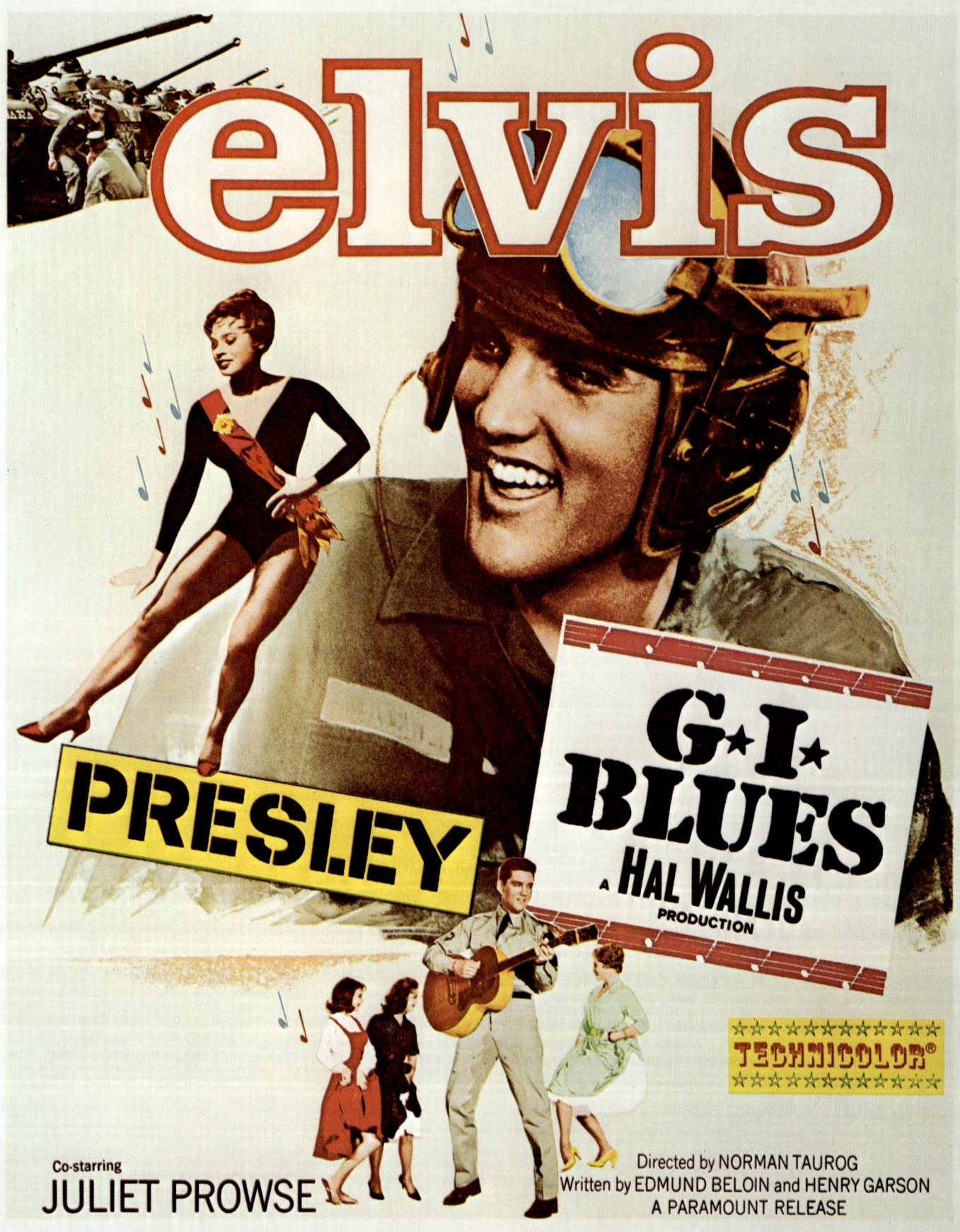

A Paramount Picture (1960)

Cast

Elvis Presley, Juliet Prowse, James Douglas, Robert Ivers, Leticia Roman, Sigrid Maier, Arch Johnson

Credits

Produced by Hal B. Wallis. Directed by Norman Taurog. Associate Producer—Paul Nathan. Written by Edmund Beloin and Henry Garson.

Synopsis

Tulsa McLean (Elvis Presley), a tank gunner, Cooky (Robert Ivers), a radio man, and Rick (James Douglas), a tank driver, have formed a musical combo known as the Three Blazes to fill the off-hours of their Army tour-of-duty in West Germany. Playing pickup dates, they hope to save enough money to open a small nightclub on their return to civilian life.

When a luckless G.I. is suddenly transferred to Alaska on the eve of a campaign to win a $300 wager for himself and his buddies by spending the night with Lili (Juliet Prowse), a steam-heated cabaret dancer with a heart of ice, Tulsa is drafted to replace the departed Lothario. In a sincere effort to help his friends—and to win the wager—Tulsa puts so much heart into it that he goes beyond the call of duty by falling in love with Lili. As she shows him the sights of Frankfurt, Tulsa finds Lili to be warm and agreeable, despite her reputation. But as they fall more and more under each other's spell, little does Lili realize that they are being constantly watched by Tulsa's buddies to see that he is living up to the terms of the wager. Warming up to Tulsa, Lili invites him to her apartment. Not wanting to take advantage of her, he leaves shortly thereafter.

About this time, Tulsa is also drafted into service as baby-sitter for the newborn son of Rick and Marla (Sigrid Maier), while the pair go off to get married and legitimize their offspring. Tulsa has problems with the baby and phones Lili, who tells him to bring the baby to her apartment. And so, under very innocent circumstances, Tulsa spends the night at Lili's apartment. His buddies, stationed outside, rejoice in the belief that he has fulfilled the terms of the wager.

The following day, rehearsals are under way for a giant Armed Forces show in which Lili and the Three Blazes will appear. Tulsa's sergeant (Arch Johnson) brags of the boy's success, and Lili learns that she was only a military objective to Tulsa. Meanwhile Tulsa's commanding officer learns of the wager and attempts to reprimand him by shipping him to another base. He also feels that an apology is due Lili, who, after hearing of the wager, believes that Tulsa's baby-sitting chore was just an excuse for spending the night with her.

But Rick and Marla tell Lili that Tulsa really was doing them a favor in baby-sitting for them. Lili realizes her mistake and her love for Tulsa, confessing them to him. He confesses that he loves her, too, and that he wants to marry her, just in time for a red, white and blue finale, accompanied by the Armed Forces show.

Elvis' first film after his army hitch, *G.I. Blues* showed us Elvis with light hair and a flattop haircut. Juliet Prowse was excellent as the girl Elvis finally wins. The film was fun and the soundtrack one of the better ones. Standout songs: "G.I. Blues," "Pocketful of Rainbows" and "Didja Ever?"

right: with Juliet Prowse

A Twentieth Century-Fox Picture (1960)

Cast

Elvis Presley, Barbara Eden, Steve Forrest, Dolores Del Rio, John McIntire, Rudolpho Acosta, Karl Swenson, Ford Rainey, Richard Jaeckel, L.Q. Jones, Douglas Dick, Anne Benton, Perry Lopez, Sharon Bercutt

Credits

Produced by David Weisbart. Directed by Don Siegel. Screenplay by Clair Huffaker and Nunnally Johnson. Based on a novel by Clair Huffaker.

Synopsis

Pacer (Elvis Presley) and Clint (Steve Forrest) Burton approach their parents' ranch in the early evening. They are greeted with a surprise party for Clint's birthday by their parents, Neddy (Dolores Del Rio) and Sam (John McIntire), and their friends, Roz Pierce (Barbara Eden), Clint's fiancee, and her brother Angus (Richard Jaeckel). Also there are Tom (L.Q. Jones) and Will (Douglas Dick) Howard and their sister Dorothy (Anne Benton). Since the Howards have a ten-mile ride and the Pierces an even longer ride to The Crossing, the party breaks up early. A Kiowa war party, led by Buffalo Horn (Rudolpho Acosta), is waiting for the Howards and everyone is killed and the ranch burned.

The Burtons are discussing the tragedy that night when a posse of white men led by Dred Pierce (Karl Swenson) rides up. They demand a declaration that the Burtons are on their side. They make insulting references to Neddy as a "Kiowa squaw" that result in a shooting incident, after which the posse maliciously shoots some of the Burton cattle and scatters the rest. The Burtons are now squarely in the middle. The next day Sam and Clint ride out to round up the cattle, leaving Pacer to guard his mother. That night, two hungry trappers, driven out of the hills by Kiowas, are offered food by Pacer. While he is outside, they make humiliating advances toward Neddy. She hits one with a ladle, and they leave when Pacer untruthfully tells them that Sam and Clint have returned. Pacer intercepts them outside and beats them unmercifully.

Next morning Buffalo Horn arrives with an invitation to Pacer to join him. When Pacer refuses, he is told that his ranch will be the next to go. He and Neddy decide to go with Buffalo Horn to the Kiowa camp to try to stop this impending disaster for everyone. At the camp, Neddy finds the women fiercely against her. Pacer, however, is accepted and allowed to return home before making his decision. He and Neddy are escorted by his boyhood friend, Two Moons (Perry Lopez). Suddenly there is a shot! Will Howard, burned and in shock, has survived the massacre and is wandering the countryside, obsessed with vengeance. He kills Two Moons and badly wounds Neddy. At the ranch Sam looks after his wife with loving care. When he leaves to water the stock, she follows some deep instinct to go into the mountains in search of her "flaming star" of death. Pa sees her, and she dies in his arms. Pacer, Clint, Roz and the doctor arrive too late. In his grief, Pacer curses all those who delayed the doctor.

with Dolores Del Rio

Pacer takes the body of Two Moons back to the Kiowa encampment. There Two Moons' betrothed, Bird's Wing (Sharon Bercutt), tells him of the plan to attack The Crossing that night. In his hatred, he agrees to help but extracts a promise that his father's place will be spared. While rounding up cattle, however, Sam Burton is ambushed and killed. Clint is wounded that evening and Pacer leads the Kiowas away from his brother. Pacer is badly wounded but he manages to save Clint and bring him to The Crossing. Clint awakens in bed to find his brother terribly wounded. "Just wanted to make sure you're all right," Pacer says. "Don't try to help me. I've been killed already—just stubborn about dying." He, too, he says, has seen the "flaming star" of death and must ride into the hills to meet it.

with Dolores Del Rio

with Barbara Eden

Flaming Star probably ranks as number two in quality among Elvis' films. Again he had light hair in this dramatic role. The film was originally intended for Marlon Brando, but Elvis more than handled the role. A dramatic western, it still stands up, after all these years, with *King Creole* as the best of Elvis Presley's films.

A Twentieth Century-Fox Picture (1961)

Cast

Elvis Presley, Hope Lange, Tuesday Weld, Millie Perkins, Rafer Johnson, John Ireland, Gary Lockwood, William Mims, Raymond Greenleaf

Credits

Produced by Jerry Wald. Directed by Philip Dunne. Screenplay by Clifford Odets. Based on a novel by J. R. Salamanca.

Synopsis

Glenn Tyler (Elvis Presley), a moody and rebellious young man, is drawn into a fight with his drunken brother and seriously injures him. Thinking he has killed him, Glenn flees but is caught by police and turned over to the local court. Sitting in judgment on his case, among others, are Phil Macy (John Ireland), local wealthy lawyer-politico, and Irene Sperry (Hope Lange), a psychiatric consultant. When his own father turns against him, the court remands Glenn to the custody of his uncle. Glenn goes to work in his uncle's tonic plant and to live with his uncle, his cousin Nory (Tuesday Weld), and her baby. Betty Lee (Millie Perkins), his childhood sweetheart, visits him and tells him he can count on her.

Glenn goes to see Irene Sperry on his first probation visit. He is hostile but she wins his respect and learns that he has a strong desire to write. She wants to help him. His uncle tries to throw him and Nory together. Betty Lee's parents are disturbed at Glenn's seeming irresponsibility. Betty Lee and Glenn go to the local dance hall where Glenn tangles with Cliff Macy (Gary Lockwood), Phil Macy's son. As time goes on Glenn and Irene Sperry become friends and their consultations become tinged with emotion. Phil wants to marry Irene but is afraid to get a divorce from his ailing wife. He tells Irene that his son has a bad heart and is drinking too much and asks her to help the boy. She refuses because she is too busy working with Glenn.

Nory wants Glenn to run away with her, but he holds her off. Glenn takes a story that he has written to Irene, who sends it to a college friend in an effort to arrange a scholarship for Glenn. Glenn and Betty Lee confirm their love. She says she will wait for him to return from college. Glenn is tempted by Nory. When Betty Lee's father reprimands him, he goes wild with Nory and stops his visits to both Betty Lee and Irene. After an argument with his uncle, Glenn runs off to Betty Lee. At her suggestion they turn to Irene for help. Irene arranges through Phil to clear Glenn, and Glenn, now working in a garage and writing, gets an opportunity to visit the university, where he is encouraged. He returns with Irene during a storm, and they are thrown together, but, after a slight affair, she sends him away. Cliff has seen them at the motel where they were forced to stop and spreads rumors about them. Everyone turns against them. Glenn now runs off with Nory and gets into a fight, as a result of which Cliff dies. Town feeling runs high, until Phil testifies about Cliff's heart condition and clears Glenn of responsibility. Glenn goes off to college, with Phil sponsoring him. Aboard the train, he opens an envelope. It is his story, printed in a magazine. He weeps.

with Hope Lange

with Tuesday Weld

Wild in the Country shows Elvis in a good dramatic part. Excellent costars in Hope Lange, Tuesday Weld and Millie Perkins. Soap-opera storyline, but one of Elvis' finest performances—especially the love scene between Elvis and Hope Lange at the motel.

A Paramount Picture (1961)

Cast

Elvis Presley, Joan Blackman, Angela Lansbury, Nancy Walters, Roland Winters, John Archer, Howard McNear, Flora Hayes, Gregory Gay, Steve Brodie, Iris Adrian, Darlene Tompkins, Pamela Akert, Christian Kay, Jenny Maxwell

Credits

Produced by Hal B. Wallis. Directed by Norman Taurog. Screenplay by Hal Kanter.

Synopsis

Chad Gates (Elvis Presley) returns home to Honolulu after a two-year hitch in the army. He is determined not to do what his mother wants, which is to take a job in the family pineapple business, settle down and marry a girl of his own social position. He takes a job with a tourist agency where his girl, Maile (Joan Blackman), works, and his first assignment is escorting a group of four schoolgirls around the island, chaperoned by their pretty teacher, Abigail Prentace (Nancy Walters).

Chad takes Maile to a "welcome home" party at his house, where his father, Fred (Roland Winters), and Jack Kelman (John Archer), Fred's boss and an old family friend, greet Maile cordially, but Chad's mother, Sarah Lee (Angela Lansbury), openly resents her. Next day, Chad takes the schoolgirls on a scenic drive. Three of them are nice, normal teenagers, but the fourth, Ellie (Jenny Maxwell), is constantly rude to Chad. That night, at a hukilau, she suddenly changes and kisses him. She is furious when he calls her a youngster and tells her to behave. At a luau Chad introduces Kelman to Abigail. Ellie, meanwhile, has begun to flirt with a tipsy tourist (Steve Brodie). When he begins to respond, Chad breaks it up and a fight ensues. Chad is put in jail. After being bailed out by his father, he is fired by the tourist agent. His parents now insist that Maile is a bad influence on him and that he give her up. Instead, he leaves home. Abigail hires him to take her party to Kauai. That night, after sightseeing, Ellie comes to his room and makes advances to him, just as his phone rings. It is Maile, who has just arrived with Jack Kelman. Chad tells her he'll dress and meet her in the lobby. But, before he can get rid of Ellie, two of the other girls come looking for her.

A showdown is postponed by a rap on the door from Abigail. Chad motions the three girls out the back door, then lets her in. In an ecstatic mood, she confesses she's in love. Thinking she means him, Chad tries to get her to lower her voice by moving closer to her. Ellie misinterprets his intentions as she watches through the window and runs away crying. Maile, tired of waiting, walks to his room, misunderstands the scene also and flees to her room. The other two girls return to Chad's room and tell him Ellie has driven away in a jeep. He follows her in another car and soon finds her, weeping under a tree beside the wrecked jeep. After making sure she's not hurt, he gives her a lecture and a spanking.

The next morning, Maile avoids Chad, who is avoiding Abigail. But Abigail corners him and finishes what she tried to tell him the night before: she's in love with Kelman, not him. Chad tells Maile, who, after some doubts, finally believes him.

When they all return to Honolulu, Chad, with a sly assist from Kelman, sells his father on the idea of holding the next convention of mainland employees of his company on the island. The tourist agency he plans to open after he marries Maile will handle all the arrangements.

left and above: with Joan Blackman

The biggest film of Elvis' career, its soundtrack has sold over six million dollars' worth of LPs. The scenery was quite beautiful and the soundtrack excellent. Elvis, who had brown hair, gave a good performance. Although the film was a financial success, I wish it had never been made. It was the first Presley film to feature too many songs and to have Elvis sing every time you blinked. It seems to have marked the beginning of a series of films with less plot, less originality — what would quickly become known as the Elvis Presley film.

A United Artists Picture (1962)

Cast

Elvis Presley, Arthur O'Connell, Anne Helm, Joanna Moore,
Jack Kruschen, Simon Oakland, Gavin and Robert Koon, Pam Ogles

Credits

Produced by David Weisbart. Directed by Gordon Douglas. Screenplay by
Charles Lederer. Based on a novel by Richard Powell.

Synopsis

Pop Kwimper (Arthur O'Connell) has one son, Toby (Elvis Presley), and four unofficially adopted children: three-year-old Ariadne (Pam Ogles); eight-year-old twins Eddy and Teddy (Gavin and Robert Koon) and pretty Holly (Anne Helm), who is nineteen and very much in love with Toby.

Traveling through a southern state in an ancient car, they run out of gas on an unopened stretch of highway and spend the night on the beach. When the governor (Harry Holcombe) opens the road next day, they tell him they have decided to homestead there! Their claims prove to be legal. They rent fishing poles and sell bait to passers-by and soon replace their original lean-to with a shack. They add rowboats as business improves and eventually attract other homesteaders. When gamblers Nick and Carmine (Simon Oakland and Jack Kruschen) discover that the homestead is outside both municipal and county jurisdiction, they move their huge trailer there. It houses a floating crap game. The crowd it attracts and noise from their "casino" keep the community up all night, and Toby is elected sheriff to keep the peace.

In his naiveté, Toby fails to realize that the gangsters intend at first to beat him up . . . and then to kill him. Using Army-learned judo, he overcomes the hoods who attack him, disarms the killers brought in later to shoot him, and finally routs the terrified gangsters altogether.

Meanwhile, State Welfare Superintendent Claypoole (Joanna Moore) has fallen for Toby while investigating the family. But the boy is shy, and when he spurns her she turns against him. She institutes proceedings to seize the children, claiming they are improperly cared for and, in addition, being brought up in a bad moral climate. She suggests that Toby and Holly have more than a sibling relationship. Waiving the right to legal council, the Kwimpers plead their own cases in a humorous and heart-warming scene, and the judge dismisses the action, commending the Kwimpers as hardy pioneers.

That night, for the first time, Holly exchanges her usual blue jeans for a lovely and very feminine white dress and comes to Toby, who is singing a ballad on the front porch. When he finishes, they embrace.

with Anne Helm

Follow That Dream was Elvis' best comedy. Costarring the lovely Anne Helm, it featured excellent acting and a soundtrack to match. A fun picture for every member of the family.

THE LAZY YEARS

By mid-1962 Elvis' movies had become standardized to the point where they were being referred to as the Elvis Presley Movie. The plots were all the same and the only thing that seemed to matter was that Elvis be surrounded by pretty girls and nice location shots and be able to sing twelve new songs. Essentially, the films were all fantasies, totally unrelated to reality. The films had two other things in common: all were attacked by the critics and all were winners at the box-office. It is to Elvis' credit that these films are even mildly enjoyable. Only Elvis, with so little to work with, could still fill the theaters film after film. His films also gave many fine actresses their first film break. Among them were Anne Helm, Raquel Welch, Michele Carey, Stella Stevens, Ursula Andress, Joan Blackman, Lynn Kellog, Dolores Hart, Juliet Prowse and Ann-Margret. Although Ann-Margret was already a star, *Viva Las Vegas* established her as a superstar.

Kissin' Cousins was shot in eighteen days. Once the studios realized that they could take Elvis and do a film that quickly, the "quickie" Elvis film was here to stay. Elvis was never used to his full potential in these films. Producers figured it was good enough because it was Elvis and in color. Gerald Drayson Adams, who wrote *Kissin' Cousins* and *Harum Scarum,* had this to say: "There never were any story conferences." They consisted of money first, second and third act. Colonel Parker made all the arrangements.

Bosley Crowther of the *New York Times* was one of the many who felt Elvis' acting ability was being wasted. Yvonne Craig said she'd seen only one other actor more at ease while doing a scene—Spencer Tracy. Perhaps so, but the Colonel was sure that there were a quarter of a million dyed-in-the-wool Elvis fans who'd see every picture three times, that Elvis transcended any material given to him. This point was an important one. Elvis actually did transcend all of the terrible material he was assigned. When lines formed outside theaters, those in the lines were there to see Elvis, and no one or anything else.

After finishing *Harum Scarum,* Elvis told director Gene Nelson, "There were some pretty funny things in that script. I'm gonna have to read it someday." He wasn't smiling. By this time Elvis had become the highest paid entertainer in history. He was getting one million dollars per picture . . . plus 50% of the profits! The films didn't need titles. They could have been numbered and they still would have sold. By the beginning of 1962, all of his films were fun pictures. United Artists and the Colonel chose *Kid Galahad,* a classic of the screen, for Elvis to remake. In the film, the wounds come from the makeup department but the action comes from Elvis, Gig Young and Lola Albright.

For his second film of 1962, Elvis went back to Paramount for *Girls! Girls! Girls!* Once again, the plot was the same—plenty of girls, lots of songs. Elvis' next film was *It Happened at the World's Fair.* In the film, Joan O'Brien was the girl he wanted, but she was more interested in her job at the World's Fair. Add ten forgettable songs and little Vicky Tiu and you have the idea for this 1963 movie. Elvis went south of the border for Paramount's *Fun in Acapulco.* He teamed with Ursula Andress for his visit to the jet set's favorite playground.

Elvis' first movie of 1964 was MGM's *Kissin' Cousins.* There were two Elvises in this one, the dark-haired Elvis from the army and his blond hillbilly cousin, also Elvis. Elvis' next film was also an MGM product. This film is the best Elvis flick of this period. Elvis was a romantic swinger, and the girl he romanced was Ann-Margret. *Viva Las Vegas* was full of songs, dances and that little something extra—maybe because Ann and Elvis were so fond of each other in real life that it couldn't help but come across on the screen.

For his sixteenth role, Elvis was back at Paramount to star in *Roustabout.* There were thrills and spills, fights and love scenes, all set against the colorful life of a carnival. Elvis starred with Barbara Stanwyck and Joan Freeman. Raquel Welch made a brief appearance in a bit part. *Girl Happy,* his next film, took him back to MGM. Fans loved it, as usual, and it did big business at the box-office. Physical fitness was part of the idea in *Tickle Me,* with Elvis showing the girls at a resort how to stay in shape. Elvis' costar in this Allied Artists picture was the beautiful Jocelyn Lane, who bore a striking resemblance to Brigitte Bardot.

After *Tickle Me,* it was back to MGM for *Harum Scarum.* MGM was thinking of Rudolph Valentino. If he could do it, why couldn't Elvis? The film took Elvis to the exotic East for romance, run-ins with sultans and time to sing eleven songs. Mary Ann Mobley and Fran Jeffries shared top billing with Elvis. The song "Frankie and Johnny" had always been a favorite of Elvis'. When United Artists discussed it as a project for a film, Elvis approved. The result was a movie set in the good old days, with the chips, fists and songs flying. Elvis' fans were surprised to find him wearing ruffled shirts and silk scarves, but they loved every moment of the movie—and all of the songs Elvis introduced in it. Paramount's *Paradise—Hawaiian Style* seemed like an unsuccessful remake of *Blue Hawaii.* Elvis could do little with this weak script. Many of his fans mentioned that he was beginning to look tired and overweight.

MGM's *Spinout* was a big improvement. Elvis looked great and the film featured Elvis' best soundtrack since *Blue Hawaii.* In *Easy Come, Easy Go,* Elvis once again worked with Hal Wallis, although this film wasn't nearly as successful as their past efforts.

with Joan O'Brien

with Vernon Presley and Mark King

Double Trouble was the title of MGM's new Elvis film. It provided Elvis with a change-of-pace setting as well as the opportunity to display his comedy skills. Annette Day shared top billing, and she and Elvis became very close friends. Elvis' next film was *Clambake,* a good-time film in the now familiar formula. Back to MGM to star in *Stay Away, Joe.* Elvis looked great as a half-Indian rodeo champ. In this comedy, Elvis would rather kiss than scalp anyone. The film was a step in the right direction. His costars were Katy Jurado, Joan Blondell and Burgess Meredith.

Before beginning work on MGM's *Speedway*, America's favorite bachelor took the step. On May 1, 1967, it happened. At 9:30 in the morning the couple all America had been watching for years stood in front of Nevada Supreme Court Justice David Zenoff and said their "I do's." They waltzed to the strains of "Love Me Tender," toasted by eighty-eight invited guests. Millions of young girls, Elvis' ardent fans, cried with jealousy. One lovely young woman, now Mrs. Elvis Presley, cried with joy.

Instead of taking a honeymoon, Elvis went back to work. Playing opposite Elvis in *Speedway* was Nancy Sinatra, a friend of many years. The plot was the same as most of the films of the lazy years, with models adding glamor and Elvis adding songs. MGM next produced *Live a Little, Love a Little.* There were plenty of laughs, with a takeoff on "bunny clubs" and a gigantic Great Dane who would have stolen the picture if the beautiful Michele Carey hadn't played opposite Elvis.

By this time the Presley film was beginning to tire and the box-office receipts began to dwindle. It was obvious that a change would have to be made.

A United Artists Picture (1962)

Cast

Elvis Presley, Gig Young, Lola Albright, Joan Blackman, Charles Bronson, Ned Glass, Robert Emhardt, David Lewis, Michael Dante, Judson Pratt

Credits

Produced by David Weisbart. Directed by Phil Karlson. Screenplay by William Fay. Based on a story by Francis Wallace.

Synopsis

Back from the army, Walter Gulick (Elvis Presley) becomes a sparring partner at a fighters' training camp owned by Willy Grogan (Gig Young). Walter is not a very good boxer, but he can absorb a great deal of punishment and he has a powerful right hand, with which he knocks out Joie Shakes (Michael Dante). Willy immediately sees a fortune in Walter, and he sorely needs the money to pay off a gambling debt to Otto Danzig (David Lewis), a gangster. Danzig has left two of his hoods at the camp to watch Willy and make sure that he doesn't talk to the police about a crime he was involved in.

Willy's sister Rose (Joan Blackman) arrives to stay at the camp and almost immediately falls for Walter. After several fights, all of which he wins by spectacular knockouts with his powerhouse right, Walter proposes to Rose and they plan to marry as soon as he quits the ring and goes into business with a local garage owner. Willy, however, is against their romance because of his low opinion of fighters.

When Danzig overmatches Walter with one of his own fighters, far out of Walter's class, Willy's girl, Dolly (Lola Albright), accuses him of overmatching Walter for spite and leaves him. On the eve of the fight, Danzig offers Walter's trainer, Lew Nyack (Charles Bronson), five hundred dollars not to work in Walter's corner, because he wants to put his own "cut-man" there to make sure Walter's cuts stay open. When Lew refuses, the hoods break all his fingers. Arriving before they leave, Willy attacks them in the locker room and is joined in a free-for-all by Walter. Together they overcome the hoods.

The night of the fight, Walter KOs his opponent and his dressing room is the scene of happy confusion. He will marry Rose; Willy and Dolly will marry also.

with Charles Bronson

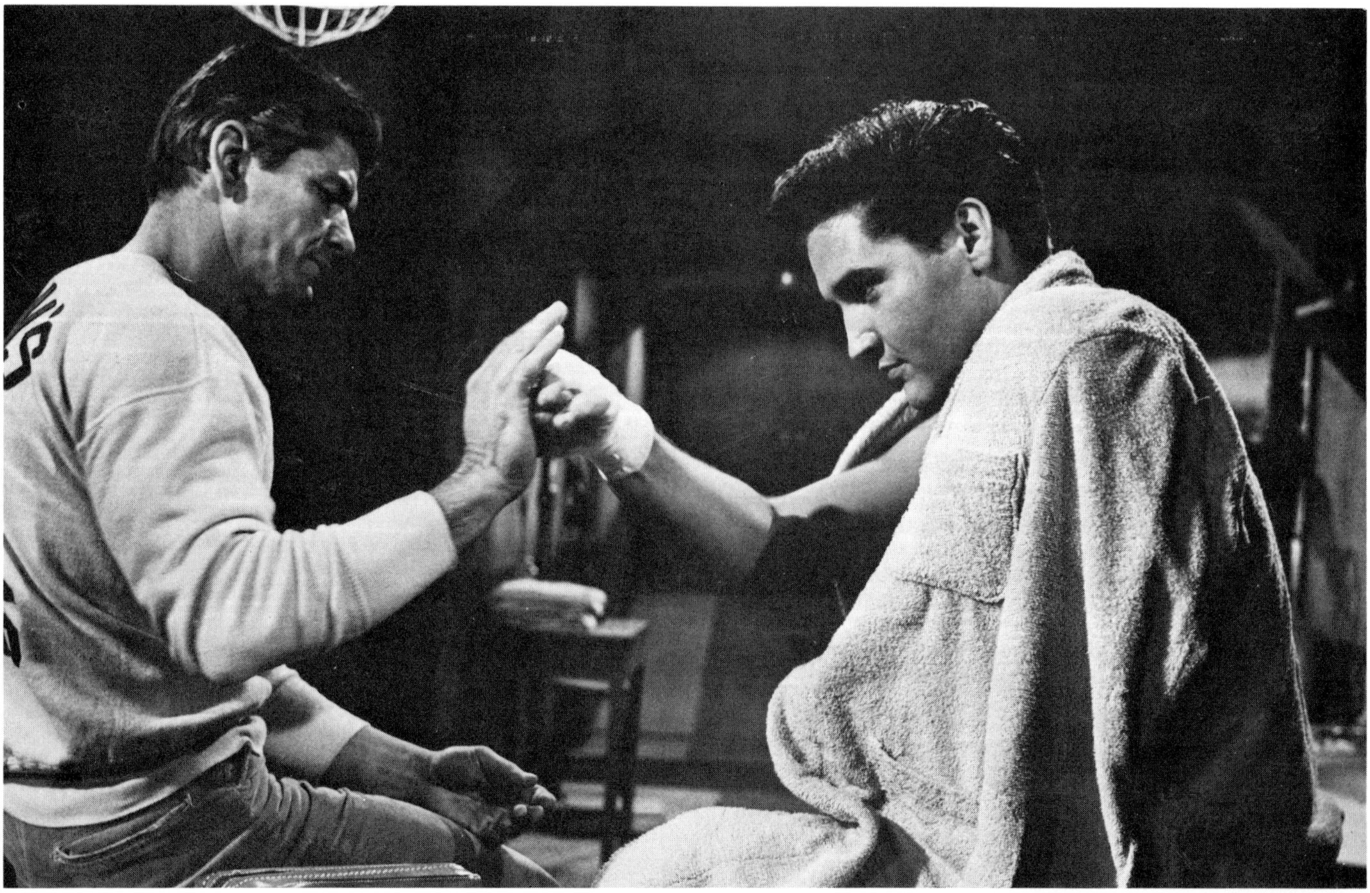

with Joan Blackman

Kid Galahad mixed drama, comedy and music well. By no means an excellent film, it nevertheless remains quite enjoyable. The soundtrack had only one standout song, "King of the Whole Wide World."

A Paramount Picture (1962)

Cast

Elvis Presley, Stella Stevens, Jeremy Slate, Laurel Goodwin, Frank Puglia

Credits

Produced by Hal Wallis. Directed by Norman Taurog. Screenplay by Edward Anhalt and Allan Weiss from a story by Allan Weiss.

Synopsis

Ross Carpenter (Elvis Presley) is skipper of a charter fishing boat for Alexander Stavros (Frank Puglia), a genial Greek who also owns a sailboat called the *West Wind*. Ross and his father had built the boat just before his father's death. Ross lives aboard the *West Wind,* which Stavros has agreed to sell back to him when he has saved enough. But Stavros is forced to take his ailing wife to Arizona and tells Ross he must reluctantly sell everything, including the boat, in order to move. Robin (Stella Stevens), a singer in a local club, is Ross' girl, but she realizes his first love is the *West Wind.* After a clash with a heckler at the club, Ross meets the heckler's companion, lovely Laurel Dodge (Laurel Goodwin), and makes a lunch date with her. Unavoidably late for the date, Ross finds Laurel sitting with an older man and leaves angrily. The next day Laurel explains to Ross that the older man was her father and they arrange a dinner date. Robin arrives as Laurel is leaving and is hurt by Ross' suggestion that they just be "good friends." Ross takes Laurel sailing next day and tells her about his dream of owning the *West Wind.* When a storm threatens, they take shelter in Paradise Cove, at the home of Kin and Madame Yung, the parents of his first mate, Chen Yung. That night Laurel tells Ross she is trying to get over a bad romance and is afraid to fall in love again. After the storm, they return to find that Stavros has sold the boat to Wesley Johnson (Jeremy Slate), a boat broker and a tough customer. Despite his instant antagonism, Ross goes to work for Johnson on one of his tuna boats. Johnson infuriates Ross by nearly doubling the price of the *West Wind* and putting it up for sale to the highest bidder.

To raise the money, Ross takes a job singing in the same nightclub as Robin. His popularity makes Robin angry and hurt. Laurel gets herself a job and a small apartment, where their romance blossoms. With money from her wealthy father, Laurel buys the *West Wind,* warning Johnson not to tell Ross who bought it. Ross catches Johnson trying to cheat him and a fight ensues. It ends abruptly, however, when Ross notices that the "For Sale" sign has been removed from his boat. With his boat sold, all the fight goes out of him. Moved by his grief, Laurel admits that she is the new owner and that she bought it for him. She confesses that she has kept her wealth a secret because, until Ross came along, all the men who attracted her were after her money.

But her fond intentions backfire, due to Ross' violent aversion to anything remotely resembling charity. After his father's death, Ross had to accept help and has hated the idea ever since. After an angry, embarrassed attempt to explain this to Laurel, Ross walks away leaving her very unhappy. Later, Laurel seeks out Robin, tells her what has happened and humbly asks her where Ross might have gone. At first Robin is vengefully pleased by Laurel's plight but, when she realizes that she is no longer in love with Ross herself, she suggests to Laurel that "when he gets into a mood he just disappears and, now that the Stavroses have gone, he's probably at Paradise Cove with the Yungs."

Laurel has a boat to get there but no one to sail it. She asks Johnson, who willingly agrees. As they set off in the *West Wind* Chen recognizes them and calls Ross on the radio phone. They both think that Laurel is in trouble and Ross hurries to rescue her in a motorboat. He boards the *West Wind* and, before anyone can explain, he knocks down Johnson and makes him agree to buy the boat back from Laurel. That night, at a huge colorful party at Paradise Cove, Ross revises his plans for the future and asks a very happy Laurel to marry him.

with Laurel Goodwin and Stella Stevens

Great title song, poor film, a very weak plot. We have Elvis with black hair singing every few minutes. Definitely the pattern for the Presley formula film had begun. An excellent soundtrack, highlighted by "Return to Sender."

A Metro-Goldwyn-Mayer Picture (1963)

Cast

Elvis Presley, Joan O'Brien, Gary Lockwood, Vicky Tiu, H. M. Wynant, Edith Atwater, Guy Raymond, Dorothy Green, Kam Tong, Yvonne Craig

Credits

Produced by Ted Richmond. Directed by Norman Taurog.
Screenplay by Si Rose and Seaman Jacobs.

Synopsis

Mike Edwards (Elvis Presley) and his sidekick Danny Burke (Gary Lockwood) are a couple of bush pilots who have their ups and downs financially as well as aeronautically. Mike has a weakness for women and Danny is a compulsive gambler. Between them, they are usually broke. At the moment, they hope to achieve solvency by working in the potato fields of Washington as crop dusters.

Soon, however, the sheriff serves them with a writ attaching their plane for bills owed. They try to hitchhike to anyplace where they can get a job. They get a ride from a Chinese farmer (Kam Tong) and his little niece Sue-Lin (Vicky Tiu), who are on their way to the Seattle World's Fair.

When they arrive in Seattle, little Sue-Lin breaks out in tears when some unexpected business makes it impossible for her uncle to take her to the fair. Mike volunteers to escort the child, while Danny finds a shady old friend, Bradley (H. M. Wynant), who can help the boys out of their financial mess. Mike and Sue-Lin go on all the rides and Sue-Lin samples all the food. When she gets a stomachache, Mike takes her to the dispensary. While there, he fakes an illness of his own in order to meet a lovely nurse, Diane Warren (Joan O'Brien). Mike can't get to first base.

In the meantime, Danny wins a housetrailer for them to stay in. The next day, the boys take a skywriting job. The results are disastrous. Mike goes to see Diane and this time gets a dinner date. Mike and Diane have a fight and Sue-Lin tearfully reports that her uncle has disappeared. Mike takes her back to the trailer and sings her to sleep. The next day, sensing that Mike is lovesick for Diane, Sue-Lin arranges a reunion by pretending to be sick. The romance again hits the rocks when child welfare takes Sue-Lin into custody and Mike learns that Diane was the one who turned in the report.

Danny's hoodlum friend has managed to get their plane out of hock in exchange for the boys' flying some freight to Canada. Just as they are about to take off, Mike learns that Sue-Lin has escaped from the welfare board. He manages to find her at the fair and brings her to the airport with him. When Bradley gets violent over the child's being there, Mike gets suspicious and peeks into one of the cargo boxes. It is loaded with furs, which Bradley is trying to smuggle out of the country. It's a battle royal then, with Mike, Danny and the law winning. There is more good news as Sue-Lin's uncle returns and Mike learns that it was Danny and not Diane who reported Sue-Lin to the welfare board. Arm in arm, Mike and Diane make another trip to the fair. They love each other and they love their country, too. They'll be together as volunteers in the space program.

with Yvonne Craig

with Vicky Tiu

Elvis dressed to kill and looking handsome. *It Happened at the World's Fair* contains all the Elvis trademarks of pretty girls, songs, laughs, fights and lots of nice World's Fair scenes. The songs were well integrated into the action of the film.

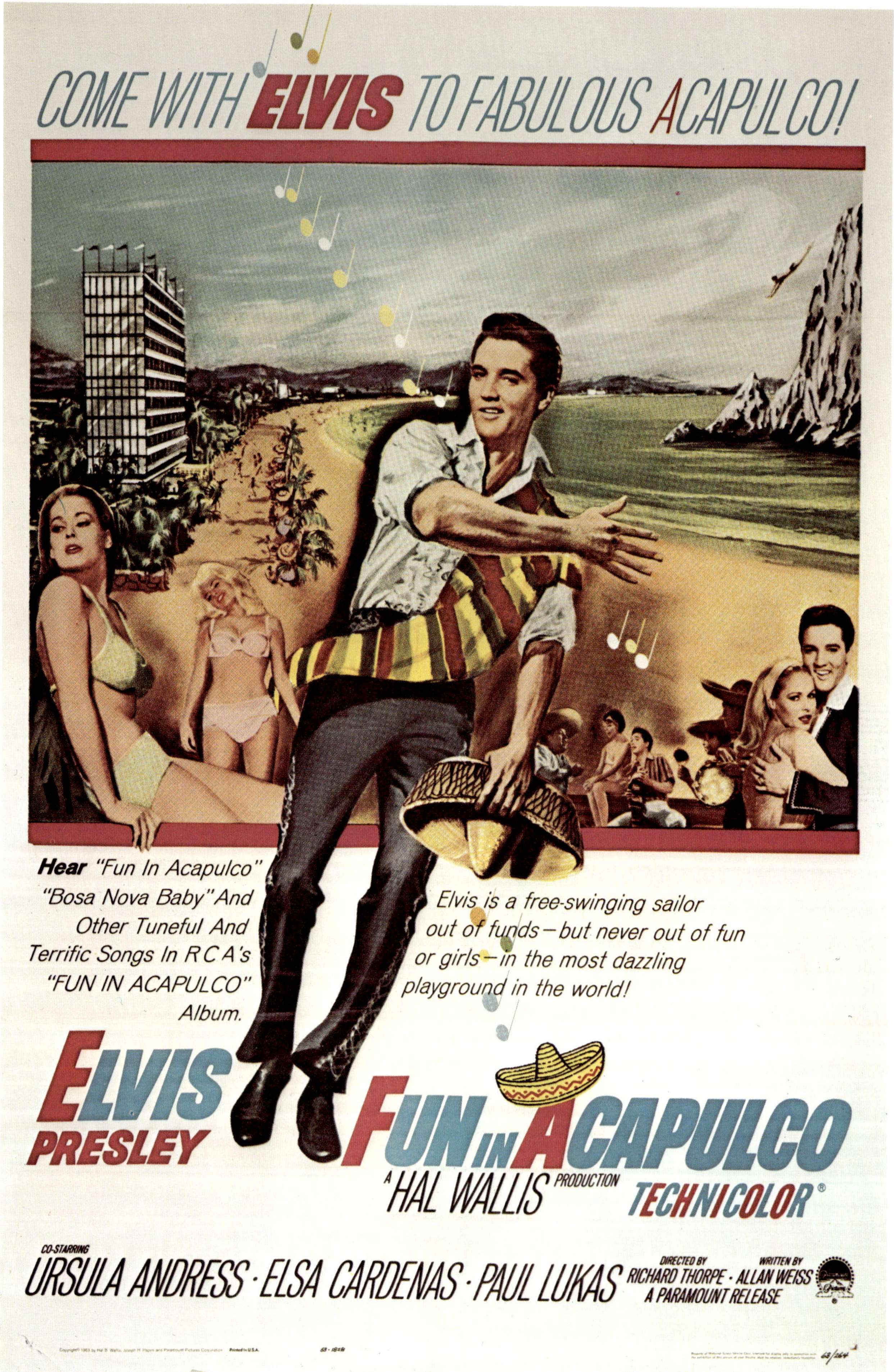
COME WITH ELVIS TO FABULOUS ACAPULCO!
Hear "Fun In Acapulco" "Bosa Nova Baby" And Other Tuneful And Terrific Songs In R C A's "FUN IN ACAPULCO" Album.
Elvis is a free-swinging sailor out of funds—but never out of fun or girls—in the most dazzling playground in the world!
ELVIS PRESLEY
FUN IN ACAPULCO
A HAL WALLIS PRODUCTION
TECHNICOLOR®
CO-STARRING
URSULA ANDRESS · ELSA CARDENAS · PAUL LUKAS
DIRECTED BY RICHARD THORPE · WRITTEN BY ALLAN WEISS
A PARAMOUNT RELEASE
Copyright © 1963 by Hal B. Wallis, Joseph H. Hazen and Paramount Pictures Corporation
Printed in U.S.A.

A Paramount Picture (1963)

Cast

Elvis Presley, Ursula Andress, Elsa Cardenas, Paul Lukas, Larry Domasin, Alejandro Rey, Robert Carricart, Teri Hope

Credits

Produced by Hal B. Wallis. Directed by Richard Thorpe.
Screenplay by Allan Weiss.

Synopsis

Mike Windgren (Elvis Presley) arrives in Acapulco as a sailor on a motor yacht. He is escaping from a tragic incident in the States where, as a trapeze artist, he caused his partner to be seriously injured. A young shoeshine boy named Raoul (Larry Domasin) hears Mike sing and volunteers to become his manager. Raoul is related to practically everyone in the city and succeeds in getting Mike hired as a singer in a resort hotel, where he soon becomes involved with two beautiful women: Dolores Gomez (Elsa Cardenas), a lady bullfighter, and Margarita Dauphine (Ursula Andress), the hotel's social director. Slowly he finds himself more and more attracted to Margarita.

In addition to singing every night, Mike also works as a lifeguard at the hotel swimming pool. The regular lifeguard, Moreno (Alejandro Rey), likes Margarita and resents Mike. One day Mike tries to dive from the high board but cannot, because he remembers that fateful day when he dropped his circus partner. Moreno notices Mike's fear of heights and, after some sleuthing, discovers the true story. He decides to use this information to win back Margarita.

Every night Moreno does a spectacular dive off the cliffs of La Quebrada—136 feet into the raging surf. One evening, Moreno and Mike have an argument, which turns into a brawl. Mike wins, and Moreno pretends to be too hurt to do his nightly dive.

Mike decides to overcome his fear of heights and make the dive himself. Slowly and dramatically, he climbs the rock cliffs and—after a moment of hesitation—cuts the water in a perfect dive. As the onlookers applaud him wildly, Mike rushes out of the water to embrace Margarita and Raoul. Triumphant at having conquered his fear of heights, Mike proposes that they all go to Florida . . . and Margarita and Raoul happily consent to go.

Fun in Acapulco was a film that left most fans satisfied. A vast improvement on most of the films that went before, such as *Girls! Girls! Girls!* and *It Happened at the World's Fair.* The soundtrack contained the fantastic ballad "El Toro" and the hit "Bossa Nova Baby." The performance of the latter was the most exciting scene in the film. There was quite a bit more drama in this film than most of Elvis' musicals.

with Ursula Andress and Elsa Cardenas

A Metro-Goldwyn-Mayer Picture (1964)

Cast

Elvis Presley, Arthur O'Connell, Glenda Farrell,
Jack Albertson, Pam Austin, Cynthia Pepper, Yvonne Craig,
Donald Woods, Tommy Farrell, Beverly Powers, Robert Stone

Credits

Produced by Sam Katzman. Directed by Gene Nelson. Screenplay by Gerald Drayson Adams and Gene Nelson. Story by Gerald Drayson Adams.

Synopsis

It is the intention of the U.S. Air Force to build a gigantic missile base at the very top of a mountain in Tennessee called Big Smoky. The owner of the mountain is a hillbilly moonshiner by the name of Pappy Tatum (Arthur O'Connell). He doesn't want anyone on his mountain because he believes they are from Internal Revenue and that they will confiscate his still. Together with his wife, Ma Tatum (Glenda Farrell), and their two daughters, Selina (Pam Austin) and Azalea (Yvonne Craig), and also with the help of Jodie (Elvis Presley), a nephew, they manage to ward off visitors.

Air Force officials decide upon a different method of approach. They contact an enlisted man from Tennessee—2nd Lt. Josh Morgan (Elvis Presley), who they think will be able to make more headway, since he was born some fifteen miles from Big Smoky mountain. Josh is assigned to work with Captain Robert Salbo (Jack Albertson), and together they must obtain Pappy's signature for the lease of his property.

They arrive along with a squadron at Big Smoky mountain, where they are captured by the Tatums. Then it happens. Josh meets Jodie and, to everyone's utter amazement, they turn out to be the living image of one another. With one difference—one is blond and the other dark. Josh explains the reason for this—his greataunt married a Tatum, and so they hit on the happy solution that they're all kissin' cousins!

Both of Pappy's daughters keep chasing Josh. In the meantime Jodie falls for an Air Force typist. Josh and Salbo finally get Pappy to sign the agreement. One of the clauses in the agreement states that a special police patrol will keep all trespassers from Pappy's land. This will also prevent the Internal Revenue from breaking up his still, which was his main concern all along.

below: with Yvonne Craig and Pam Austin

left: with Yvonne Craig and Cynthia Pepper

The beginning of the "quickie" Elvis film. Although the film was enjoyable, it contained more than just touches of *Follow That Dream*. There were two Elvises in the film—the blond-wigged Jodie and the black-haired Josh. The soundtrack was very good, and the title song was different than the single release.

A Metro-Goldwyn-Mayer Picture (1964)

Cast

Elvis Presley, Ann-Margret, Cesare Danova,
William Demarest, Nicky Blair

Credits

Produced by Jack Cummings and George Sidney. Screenplay by
Sally Benson. Directed by George Sidney.

Synopsis

Lucky Jackson (Elvis Presley) has one ambition—to be the world's racing champion. To achieve this, he and his mechanic, Shorty Farnsworth (Nicky Blair), are on their way to Las Vegas to enter their car in the annual Grand Prix. Lucky has won a considerable amount of money in a gambling saloon to enable him to do this. Arriving in Vegas, Lucky meets Count Elmo Mancini (Cesare Danova), the Italian racing champion, who is preparing his Ferrari for the big race. Lucky turns down Mancini's offer, which involves taking the other cars out of competition by hard driving so that Mancini can win with little effort.

Their minds are taken off racing when a young lovely named Rusty Martin (Ann-Margret) asks them to fix her sports car. Lucky tries to delay her by loosening a wire, but Mancini fixes the car and Rusty is on her way before Lucky can learn her name. Guessing that she's a showgirl, Lucky and Mancini begin a tour of the fabulous Las Vegas strip. But after viewing hundreds of chorus girls, they still haven't located Rusty. The next morning, Lucky finds her by accident—she is the swimming instructor at the hotel where he is staying. The reunion is a happy one for Lucky—until he falls into the pool and the money he and Shorty were going to use for a racing engine is sucked down the drain. To pay his hotel bill, he and Shorty become waiters. This makes them eligible to compete for $2,500 in prizes at the annual Employees' Talent Competition.

On his first day off, Lucky and Rusty have their first date and fall in love. On the night of the talent show, Lucky wins first prize, edging out Rusty. But, instead of winning cash, Lucky receives a gold cup and a honeymoon in Monaco. Rusty wants Lucky to give up racing because she fears he will get himself killed. She tries to win him over through jealousy by carrying on with the Count. Their candlelight dinner is turned into a riot when Lucky substitutes for the hotel's regular waiter.

Finally, just hours before the big race, the money turns up for Lucky's engine (secretly financed by Rusty's father) thanks to Rusty's inadvertent help. Lucky's car makes the starting gate on time and, in a wild and furious race, Lucky wins and returns to marry Rusty.

with Ann-Margret

If it hadn't been for the final scene of *Viva Las Vegas*, Elvis would have been in danger of losing the limelight to Miss Ann-Margret. She played an exceptionally good part and thoroughly succeeded in portraying it to the hilt. The song and dance scenes were excellent. Elvis and Ann-Margret made a fabulous duo. Good soundtrack!

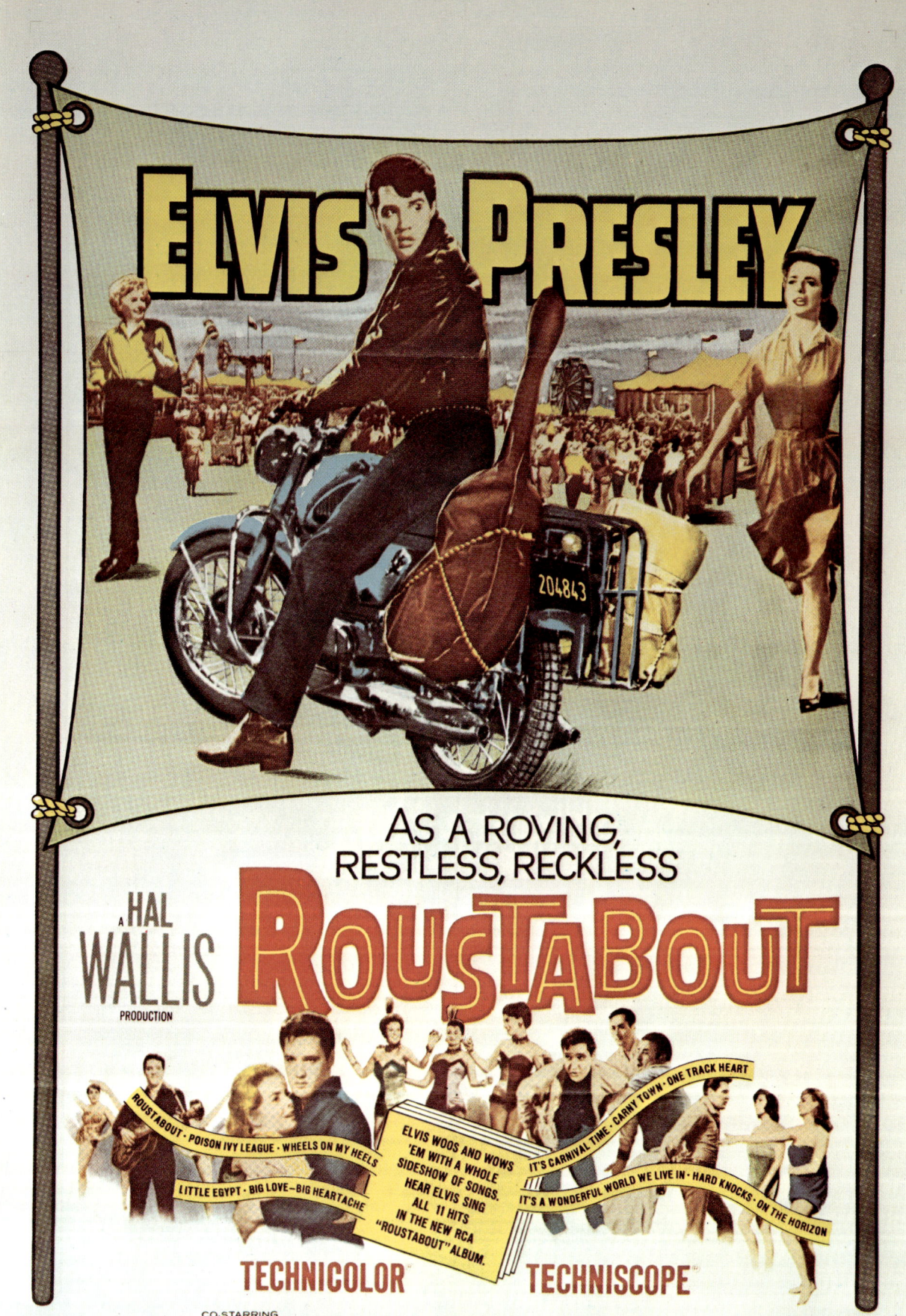

A Paramount Picture (1964)

Cast

Elvis Presley, Barbara Stanwyck, Joan Freeman, Leif Erickson, Sue Ane Langdon, Pat Buttram, Joan Staley

Credits

Produced by Hal B. Wallis. Directed by John Rich. Screenplay by Anthony Lawrence and Allan Weiss. Based on a story by Allan Weiss.

Synopsis

At Mother's Tea House, Charlie Rogers (Elvis Presley) sings pointed lyrics to student customers in order to expose their vulnerabilities. Charlie is warned by pretty waitress Marge (Joan Staley) to lay off three certain fellows who seem annoyed at his remarks. Charlie refuses to stop, and they accost him after the show; after letting them make the first move, Charlie finishes them off with a dazzling display of karate. Because of this occurrence, Charlie heads off for parts unknown on his motorcycle. After wandering for a bit, Charlie gets a job at a carnival run by Maggie Morgan (Barbara Stanwyck). He hires on as a "roustabout"—a sort of handyman.

At the carnival, Charlie meets beautiful Cathy Lean (Joan Freeman), daughter of embittered Joe Lean (Leif Erickson), who is infuriated at Charlie's interest in her. Business at the carnival is practically nonexistent, so, in between odd jobs, Charlie breaks into an impromptu song on the midway. News of this gets around and suddenly droves of young people flock to the carnival. Maggie notes this and a new career is launched for Charlie.

Things suddenly go sour for Charlie: he gets into a fight with one of the customers and, because of it, decides to leave again. Feeling that he has lost Cathy, he accepts an offer from a rival carnival and takes off. With Charlie gone, Maggie's carnival again takes a nosedive, and its creditors come knocking at the doors. As a last hope, Cathy goes to find Charlie and, at the rousing musical climax, Charlie and Cathy return to save everything, including their romance.

with Barbara Stanwyck and Joan Freeman

Not one of Elvis' better films. Although Elvis' and Barbara Stanwyck's great talent was evident, the two could not elevate the film's poor plot above mediocrity. The film does, however, contain a very enjoyable soundtrack.

A Metro-Goldwyn-Mayer Picture (1965)

Cast

Elvis Presley, Shelley Fabares, Harold J. Stone, Gary Crosby, Joby Baker, Nita Talbot, Mary Ann Mobley, Fabrizio Mioni, Jimmy Hawkins, Jackie Coogan, Peter Brooks

Credits

Produced by Joe Pasternak. Directed by Boris Sagal. Screenplay by Harvey Bullock and R. S. Allen. Story by Bullock and Allen.

Synopsis

Rusty Wells (Elvis Presley) is the leader of a combo comprising Andy (Gary Crosby), Wilbur (Joby Baker) and Doc (Jimmy Hawkins). The boys have just finished a series of dates in Chicago and, as it is Easter, they are all planning to run off to Fort Lauderdale, the teenager's holiday heaven in Florida. Because of Rusty's success at the nightclub, however, the owner, Big Frank (Harold J. Stone), decides to hold the combo over for a few weeks. Rusty finds out that Big Frank's daughter, Valerie (Shelley Fabares), is spending her Easter vacation in Fort Lauderdale and cons Big Frank into sending him and his group, full expenses paid, to keep an eagle eye on her.

When Rusty and the boys arrive at the hotel and see that Valerie is a lonely bookworm, they decide there's no need to watch her, since she appears to be interested only in reading. Rusty is sidetracked by a beautiful girl named Deena (Mary Ann Mobley) and arranges to meet her at the club where his group will be playing. While singing "Wolf Call," he spots Valerie in the audience with her date, playboy Brentwood Von Durgenfeld (Peter Brooks). He can't let Big Frank down, so he leaves Deena at the club to try to get Valerie away from Brentwood. Each time Rusty has a chance with Deena, he ends up leaving her to "rescue" Valerie. It becomes a hassle until Rusty finds himself falling in love with Valerie. When Valerie discovers that Rusty has been hired by her father as a secret chaperone, she drowns her sorrow in too many drinks and causes a sensation by doing a striptease. Rusty tries to stop her and a fight occurs, landing Valerie and her friends in jail. Rusty formulates a plan to tunnel under the jail and come up under Valerie's cell. When he gets inside her cell, he learns that Big Frank has come to town and has gotten Valerie out of jail already.

At first, Big Frank is furious and Valerie also hates Rusty. But after a talk, they both realize how fond they are of him. With romance in their eyes, Rusty and Valerie perform the last musical number together.

above: with Chris Noel, Shelley Fabares and Mary Ann Mobley

left: with Mary Ann Mobley

Elvis in a role similar to those he played in quite a few of his other films. As the title suggests, everything is lighthearted. As a musical *Girl Happy* was quite entertaining. Although the story was not very strong. Elvis' presence made it all fit together.

An Allied Artists Picture (1964)

Cast

Elvis Presley, Jocelyn Lane, Julie Adams, Jack Mullaney, Merry Anders, Connie Gilchrist, Edward Faulkner, Bill Williams, Laurie Burton, John Dennis

Credits

Produced by Ben Schwalb. Directed by Norman Taurog.
Story and Screenplay by Elwood Ullman and Edward Bernds.

Synopsis

Singing rodeo star Lonnie Beale (Elvis Presley) drifts into Zuni Wells with his guitar and is hired by Vera Radford (Julie Adams), owner of an expensive dude ranch beauty spa, where he is assigned a cottage with handyman Stanley Potter (Jack Mullaney). All the glamour girl patrons fall for the new wrangler and his singing, which means he has to lick Adonis-type swimming coach Brad Bentley (Edward Faulkner). But Pam Merritt (Jocelyn Lane), the shapely physical instructor, snubs him as a fortune hunter. She surprises a prowler in her hut and her screams bring Lonnie, but the man escapes. Deputy Sheriff Sturdivant (Bill Williams) warns that she has talked too much about a letter her grandfather wrote directing her to his hidden gold. Next day she goes to the ghost town of Silverado. Lonnie finds her in the saloon and they have fun imagining the town as it used to be.

That evening, Lonnie stops two masked men from abducting Pam. The men drive into the desert and meet Sturdivant who is angered at their bungling. Pam shows Lonnie the letter and tells him the story behind it. Later she finds him kissing Vera and will not listen to his explanations. Anguished, Lonnie leaves for the rodeo circuit, but Stanley brings him back and they find Pam in Silverado, where a sudden storm strands them all for the night. A man in a monster mask breaks into Pam's room that night, demanding the letter. Lonnie floors him, and unmasks Adolph (John Dennis), the ranch chef. Lonnie disposes of two more hoods and, together with Pam and Stanley, stumbles onto the hiding place of the gold, which cascades from a cellar wall as Sturdivant confronts them with a gun.

Lonnie and Pam fall into each other's arms. They have a wedding at the ranch and drive off, Lonnie singing to his bride and both oblivious to the fact that Stanley, trapped in a bathtub he has tied to their car, is being dragged along on the honeymoon.

with Jocelyn Lane

A very funny film. The soundtrack was composed of old songs from earlier Elvis LPs. Elvis looked great and Jocelyn Lane looked incredible. In my opinion Jocelyn was the prettiest costar Elvis ever had. The movie was fun for the entire family. In fact—although not intending to be—*Tickle Me* remains one of the best children's pictures ever.

A Metro-Goldwyn-Mayer Picture (1965)

Cast

Elvis Presley, Mary Ann Mobley, Fran Jeffries, Michael Ansara, Jay Novello, Philip Reed, Theo Marcuse, Billy Barty, Richard Reeves

Credits

Produced by Sam Katzman. Directed by Gene Nelson. Written by Gerald Drayson Adams.

Synopsis

Johnny Tyronne (Elvis Presley), a motion picture and recording star, is kidnapped while making a personal appearance tour of the Middle East. After conniving with the leader of the court entertainers, Johnny escapes over the palace walls and accidentally drops in on Princess Shalimar (Mary Ann Mobley). She tells Johnny that she is a slave girl and offers to help him in his escape. She asks Johnny why he was taken captive and he tells her that his kidnappers were planning to use him in an assassination of a very important person. The princess realizes that it has to be her father, the king (Philip Reed), that the assassins are after.

Shortly afterward, Johnny is recaptured and told that he must kill the king, or his captors will kill the court entertainers—his friends. Johnny has no choice but to do as they say. They all go to the king's palace and, while the troupe of entertainers performs, Johnny proceeds with the plan to kill the king. Just as he is about to commit murder, Shalimar appears and tells her father about the plan she learned from Johnny. Johnny now realizes that she is the king's daughter and not a slave. Johnny and the troupe wind up in the palace dungeon.

The princess is in love with Johnny even though he was going to kill her father. When night falls, Johnny again escapes and makes his way to the princess' room. He finds her there with the king and explains why he was sent to assassinate him. The princess realizes that Johnny is in love with her and they all go back to the house of the troupe leader. Sneaking in, they listen as the king's brother, Prince Dragna (Michael Ansara), tells of his plans to kill the king and inherit the throne. A battle ensues, after which the victorious king sends his brother into exile. Johnny gets to keep Princess Shalimar happily ever after.

with Mary Ann Mobley and Fran Jeffries

Harum Scarum was the weakest film of Elvis' career. Elvis looked quite handsome in his role as a kidnapped movie star, and the Arabian setting provided a change from the usual American-based story. Mary Ann Mobley was beautiful as the princess. The soundtrack from the film was completely different from anything Elvis had done in the past. The track featured the classic "So Close yet so Far Away from Paradise."

A Paramount Picture (1965)

Cast

Elvis Presley, Suzanna Leigh, James Shigeta, Marianna Hill, Donna Butterworth, Irene Tsu, Linda Wong, Julie Parrish, Jan Shepard, John Doucette, Philip Ahn, Grady Sutton

Credits

Produced by Hal B. Wallis. Executive Producer—Paul Nathan. Directed by Michael Moore. Screenplay by Allan Weiss and Anthony Lawrence. Based on an original story by Allan Weiss.

Synopsis

Rick Richards (Elvis Presley), a pilot without a job, returns to his birthplace, Hawaii. Rick hitches a ride with his pilot buddy, Danny Kohana (James Shigeta), who is flying a man named Cubberson (Grady Sutton) to a convention at the Maui Sheraton. Rick proposes that the two of them start a helicopter charter service. Danny refuses the offer, but Rick persuades a Hawaiian hostess, Lehua (Linda Wong), to send them passengers. Cubberson discovers he's at the wrong hotel—the convention is on Kauai Island. There, Rick meets another girl, Lani (Marianna Hill), whom he also persuades to send passengers. When both girls line up customers, Danny is convinced. Danrick Airways goes into business, and the owners engage Judy Hudson (Suzanna Leigh) as a secretary, nicknaming her Friday.

Rick takes off to find another girl for a passenger agent, this one at the Polynesian Cultural Center. The day's show is about to begin and Pua (Irene Tsu) coaxes Rick into it. They sing "Drums of the Islands." Next, he enlists Joanna (Julie Parrish), a Caucasian beauty working at the Kahala Hilton. While taking her for a ride, Rick loses control of the 'copter and doesn't regain it till the careening 'copter has forced a car into a ditch. Rick takes Joanna to a steak house. Friday is there with Andy Lowell (Don Collier), who becomes offensively amorous. Rick intervenes and starts a free-for-all.

The next day, Rick learns that the driver of the car was Donald Belden (John Doucette), of the Federal Aviation Agency. This means trouble. Friday tells Rick that Lani has a couple waiting on Kauai to be flown to Honolulu. But Danny has promised his daughter Jan (Donna Butterworth) a 'copter ride, and Rick substitutes by taking her along. They land in front of a surfside eating place. They're early and Lani persuades Rick to take her and Jan to Moonlight Beach. Once there, because Rick avoids her advances, Lani buries the key to the helicopter ignition. All three dig in vain. They spend the night there. Danny finds them but will not accept Rick's story and dissolves their partnership. On Rick's return, he finds that Danny and Jan have not come back. Friday blames Rick and together they search for them.

They find the 'copter down, Danny with a broken leg, and Jan all right. Danny and Rick are friends again, but both fear they may lose their licenses, since the newspapers have told the story to the aviation board. Learning that Belden is to be guest of honor at a welcoming festival, Rick decides to plead his case. Dancing with Friday, Rick is shocked to see Lehua, Lani, Pua and Joanna there too. Recognizing him, they pull him into a number with them.

After that, he finds Belden, who assures him that because of the mitigating circumstance of the rescue he will not lose his license. The happy pilot rejoins the party, singing "This Is My Heaven" directly to Friday.

left: with Marianna Hill, Suzanna Leigh, Julie Parrish and Irene Tsu

A really poor film featuring a very poor soundtrack. Elvis was the only bright spot in this boring film. If Colonel Parker thought *Paradise* could be another *Blue Hawaii,* it's quite obvious he was mistaken.

A United Artists Picture (1966)

Cast

Elvis Presley, Donna Douglas, Nancy Kovack, Sue Ane Langdon, Anthony Eisley, Harry Morgan, Audrey Christie, Robert Strauss

Credits

Produced by Edward Small. Directed by Frederick de Cordova. Screenplay by Alex Gottlieb. Based on a story by Nat Perrin.

Synopsis

Frankie (Donna Douglas) loves Johnny (Elvis Presley), but he loves gambling almost as much as he loves Frankie. She refuses to marry him until he stops betting and losing every cent he makes. Together they earn a living singing on the Mississippi gambling-showboat owned by Clint Braden (Anthony Eisley).

When a gypsy fortune teller tells Johnny that he can end his losing streak with a new redhead who is coming into his life, Johnny becomes interested. The redhead turns out to be Braden's old flame, Nellie Bly (Nancy Kovack). Frankie becomes jealous of Nellie and Braden becomes jealous of Johnny, especially when Nellie uses Johnny to try to get Braden to marry her.

Johnny's piano-playing sidekick, Cully (Harry Morgan), writes a new song called "Frankie and Johnny," which is introduced on the showboat, and it looks like Frankie and Johnny will make it big and finally go to Broadway after Mardi Gras week in New Orleans.

Just as the fortune teller predicted, Johnny wins a fortune with Nellie beside him, but Frankie angrily throws all the money away. Then Braden's dumb bodyguard, Blackie (Robert Strauss), trying to help Braden get Johnny out of Nellie's life, puts a real bullet in the gun that Frankie uses to "kill" Johnny in the finish of the song.

But the lucky cricket that Johnny wears saves his life, and Frankie decides that she loves Johnny no matter how much he gambles.

Frankie and Johnny was based on the ever-popular song, and Elvis looked fantastic in his Mississippi gambler's outfits. The plot was thin, but quite funny. Donna Douglas was delightful as Frankie. The soundtrack was very good and featured the very beautiful "Please Don't Stop Loving Me."

left: with Donna Douglas

A Metro-Goldwyn-Mayer Picture (1966)

Cast

Elvis Presley, Shelley Fabares, Diane McBain, Deborah Walley, Dodie Marshall, Jack Mullaney, Will Hutchins, Warren Berlinger, Jimmy Hawkins, Carl Betz, Cecil Kellaway, Una Merkel

Credits

Produced by Joe Pasternak. Directed by Norman Taurog. Written by Theodore J. Flicker and George Kirgo.

Synopsis

Singer Mike McCoy (Elvis Presley) travels the country with his band, composed of Les (Deborah Walley), Curly (Jack Mullaney) and Larry (Jimmy Hawkins). He enjoys the carefree life and has no intentions of marrying. But three beautiful girls have their eyes on him. Cynthia Foxhugh (Shelley Fabares) spots Mike performing in a club. Her father, Howard Foxhugh (Carl Betz), a millionaire, offers the ensemble $5,000 to perform one number at his daughter's birthday party, but the group is booked elsewhere. Foxhugh uses his influence to cancel all Mike's concerts until he entertains for Cynthia.

Another girl in Mike's life is Diana St. Clair (Diane McBain). She's a best-selling author researching her next book, *The Perfect Male,* and Mike is one of her subjects. Diana intends to marry the man who best fills her requirements for the book's title, and Mike seems to be the winner. While the romantic snares multiply, Foxhugh tries to get Mike (an outstanding racer) to drive his new Fox Five experimental car in the Santa Fe Road Race. Realizing the band is going to leave and knowing that stubborn Mike will do the opposite of what he is told, Foxhugh sends Tracy Richards (Will Hutchins), a police lieutenant, to order the group out of town. Infuriated, Mike cons Foxhugh's neighbors into taking a second honeymoon in his vintage Dusenberg. When they leave, the band moves into their home.

The day before the race, Mike throws a swinging party, where Howard becomes aware of Diana. Philip Short (Warren Berlinger) falls in love with Cynthia. Officer Richards has eyes for Les, who plays the drums. Although usually rather plain, Les comes downstairs dressed beautifully and Mike can't believe it's the same girl. The party ends with all three girls still after Mike and the three guys after the girls. Mike promises to reveal his choice after the big race.

After winning the race, Mike announces that he's made his choice—he is going to marry all three! And he does. He marries Cynthia to Philip, Diana to Howard and Les to Tracy.

with Diane McBain, Shelley Fabares and Deborah Walley

with Deborah Walley and Jimmy Hawkins

Elvis . . . looking better than in his last few films. Elvis' role as a free-spirited band leader has him in danger of being caught and tamed by three matrimony-minded women. When not singing, or being chased by the girls, Elvis races cars. Slickly directed, *Spinout* featured a good soundtrack.

A Paramount Picture (1966)

Cast

Elvis Presley, Dodie Marshall, Pat Priest, Pat Harrington,
Skip Ward, Sandy Kenyon, Frank McHugh, Elsa Lanchester, Diki Lerner

Credits

Produced by Hal B. Wallis. Associate Producer—Paul Nathan.
Directed by John Rich. Screenplay by Allan Weiss and Anthony Lawrence.

Synopsis

While deactivating an underwater mine, Navy frogman Ted Jackson (Elvis Presley) discovers a treasure chest in the hull of an old brigantine called *Port of Call.* Intrigued by the prospect of sudden wealth, he goes to Captain Jack (Frank McHugh), owner of a marine supply store and the best source of nautical lore in the area. Jack, who fears the water, tells Ted that Joe Symington can supply information about the *Port of Call,* being the only descendant of the ship's skipper.

At the Symington home, a group of way-out artists is engaged in a yoga session. Ted finds Joe, who turns out to be a gorgeous girl (Dodie Marshall). He has seen her before, dancing at the East GO-GO, a dockside discotheque in which he used to be a partner with his best friend, Judd Whitman (Pat Harrington). Joe, full-time hostess to the unemployed artists in town, says the ship carried a cargo of coffee plus a valuable chest of Spanish pieces-of-eight.

Discharged from the Navy, Ted cons Judd into helping him reclaim the fortune. As they prepare to leave for the treasure site, Captain Jack gets seasick and is replaced by Joe. When she learns their mission, she is furious. She tells Ted he's a fortune hunter just like everyone else. But she agrees to help if the money goes toward an art center for all her friends. Before the problem is resolved, a ship approaches. It belongs to beautiful playgirl Dina Bishop (Pat Priest), who is accompanied by Gil Corey (Skip Ward). Earlier the couple had seen Ted dive to work on the mine and had secretly photographed the operation. Suspicious now, Gil re-examines the photos he shot and spots the chest. Determined to get to it first, he fakes a dead battery cable and insists that Ted tow them to shore.

Gil then convinces Captain Jack that Ted is a crook, and they go to Ted's boat for Jack's diving equipment. A fight ensues and Captain Jack, confused, hurriedly takes his supplies back to the store. Both Gil and Ted must formulate new plans. Ted searches for Joe. She and Jack are old friends and she can certainly set him straight. While he is detained at the weirdest party he's ever seen, Ted's car is taken apart and made into a mobile by crazy artist Zoltan (Diki Lerner). Ted, Judd and Joe borrow Zoltan's car and race back to the shop.

Meanwhile, Dina has lured Captain Jack onto her boat, and Gil has stolen his diving gear. Too late, Jack realizes that he has been kidnapped. On his own boat, Ted finds Gil's underwater picture with the chest circled. A message reads "Finders Keepers, Lover." By the time they reach the treasure, Gil and Dina are already submerged. Underwater, a bitter struggle ends in Gil's being floated to the surface by Ted. Ted insists on splitting the money between Joe and Judd and Captain Jack, only to discover the coins are copper, not gold, and only worth about $4,000. They all decide to pool the money as a down payment on Joe's art center and Judd throws a benefit at the Easy GO-GO to raise the remainder.

with Elsa Lanchester

By the time *Easy Come, Easy Go* was released, it was obvious that the public, as well as the avid Elvis fan, had become disenchanted with this type of movie. Any other star would have drowned with storylines such as *Easy Come* featured. The film's poor soundtrack was on a par with the plot. I found myself feeling sorry for Elvis while viewing this movie.

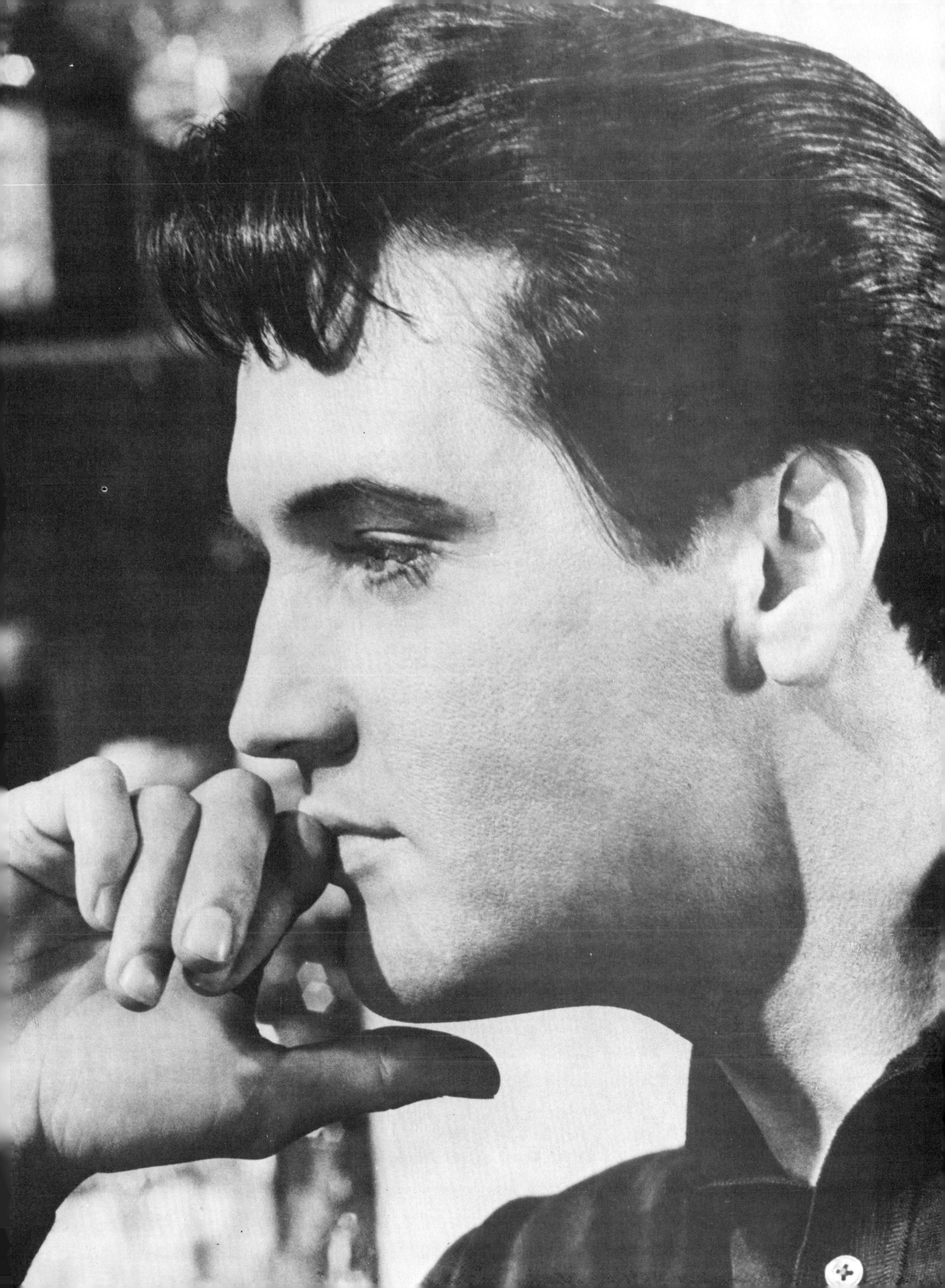

A Metro-Goldwyn-Mayer Picture (1967)

Cast

Elvis Presley, Annette Day, John Williams, Yvonne Romain,
The Wiere Brothers, Chips Rafferty, Stanley Adams, Michael Murphy, Norman Rossington,
John Alderson, Maurice Marsac, Leon Askin

Credits

Produced by Judd Bernard and Irwin Winkler. Directed by
Norman Taurog. Screenplay by Jo Heims. Based on a story
by Marc Brandel.

Synopsis

As Guy Lambert (Elvis Presley), a carefree bachelor, sings to a sea of London discotheque faces, two women enter his life. Sophisticated playgirl Claire Dunham (Yvonne Romain) is extremely enamored of Guy. Jill Conway (Annette Day) is younger but also has eyes for the entertainer.

When Jills' guardian and uncle, Gerald Waverly (John Williams), invites Guy for a visit to discuss the singer's intentions, Guy discovers that Jill is much younger than she appeared in the club. He tries to lose her but she is intent on marriage. Uncle Gerald decides to nip the romance in the bud. He has more elaborate plans for the heiress and immediately sends her off to school in Brussels, not knowing that Guy's profession is taking him there the same day.

En route to Belgium by ship, Jill searches for Guy and meets some rather strange tourists. Among them are Morley (Michael Murphy), who engages in sinister extracurricular activities; Arthur Babcock (Norman Rossington) and Archie Brown (Chips Rafferty), two bumbling smugglers looking for a fall guy, and Iceman (John Alderson), always lurking in the shadows at the moment of disaster. When a falling steamer trunk barely misses Jill, and Guy is nearly drowned, it becomes evident that someone aboard has diabolical plans for the couple. When they dock, a handful of suspicious characters are there at their heels. From Bruges to Antwerp, they miss death by a narrow margin at each turn. Babcock and Brown constantly follow Guy and Jill. Claire joins the group with a new plan of attack, and the suspicious Frenchman (Maurice Marsac) appears.

When Uncle Gerald arrives in an overprotective mood, Guy is arrested for kidnapping. Separated from Jill and unable to protect her, he calls on a good friend to hide her from danger. Instead, she is nearly asphyxiated by deadly gas. Though Guy's fellow musician George (Monty Landis) tries to help, it seems that Guy will be too late escaping from the police station to save her. No thanks to Inspector De Grotte (Leon Askin) and his men (The Wiere Brothers), everything seems to turn out all right. No one is really who he appears to be, least of all Uncle Gerald and Claire.

Thinking all is safe, Guy and Jill blissfully book passage for England, not knowing several of their mysterious friends are aboard. Thanks to Captain Roach (Stanley Adams), there is a surprise destination and an even more surprising ending in which Guy and Jill find themselves floating on a raft with a bag full of jewels.

Once again, Elvis' talents were the rock that gave this film strength. The filming of Elvis' parts was done in Hollywood; the other shots were on location in Belgium and London. The film was funny and the soundtrack fair. There were no standout songs.

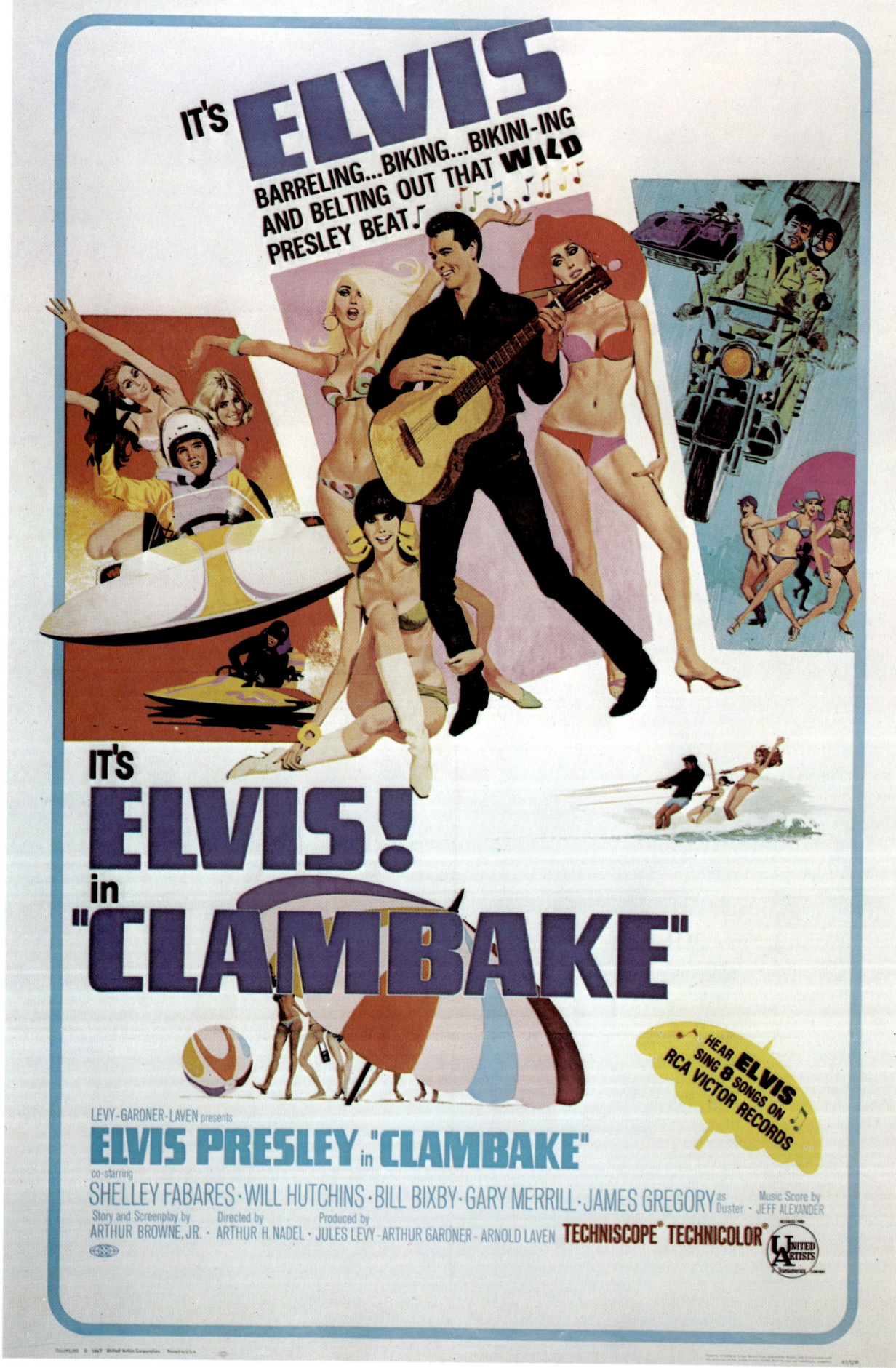

A United Artists Picture (1967)

Cast

Elvis Presley, Shelley Fabares, Will Hutchins, Bill Bixby, Gary Merrill, James Gregory, Amanda Harley, Suzy Kaye, Angelique Pettyjohn

Credits

Produced by Levy-Gardner-Laven Productions. Directed by Arthur Nadel. Story and Screenplay by Arthur Browne, Jr.

Synopsis

Heir to his father's oil millions, Scott Heyward (Elvis Presley) leaves home to see if he can accomplish something worthwhile on his own merit. En route to Miami Beach, he exchanges identities with Tom Wilson (Will Hutchins), a poor water-ski instructor. At the hotel, Wilson checks into the Presidential Suite and Scott into the employees' quarters.

His first student is pretty Dianne Carter (Shelley Fabares), who is in Miami Beach to catch a rich husband and sets her cap for James Jamison III (Bill Bixby), a rich playboy in town for the boat races. Scott is jealous when Jamison becomes interested in Dianne and tries to impress her.

Unable to fall back on his wealth, Scott forms a partnership with Sam Burton (Gary Merrill), who owns a new-design craft that mysteriously ripped apart in the previous year's race. The trouble lies with the protective coating, but Scott thinks he can help perfect it with a hardener he has developed in his father's oil lab. When he sends for the chemical, his father, Duster Heyward (James Gregory), learns of his whereabouts and flies to Florida. Here he discovers the switched identities and finally understands what is driving his son.

The formula applied to the boat requires twenty-four hours to harden, and there is no time for a test run. Scott decides to take the risk and enter the race regardless. His gamble is dangerous, but it pays off when he wins both the race and Dianne.

Even though it was formula, Elvis handled the material he had to work with very professionally. A fine soundtrack and the film's release at Christmas made it good family fun.

A Metro-Goldwyn-Mayer Picture (1968)

Cast

Elvis Presley, Burgess Meredith, Joan Blondell, Katy Jurado, Thomas Gomez, Henry Jones, L. Q. Jones, Quentin Dean

Credits

Produced by Douglas Laurence. Directed by Peter Tewksbury. Screenplay by Michael A. Hoey. Based on the novel by Dan Cushman.

Synopsis

Joe Lightcloud (Elvis Presley) persuades the local congressman to give him twenty heifers and a young bull in order to raise a herd. The congressman agrees to this as part of an experimental Indian rehabilitation project. Joe spends most of his time jumping on the backs of untamed bulls, riding a motorbike at top speed, conning merchants out of their wares, giving the local politicians headaches and refereeing fights he himself has started. Glenda Callahan (Joan Blondell), the local tavern owner, chases Joe all over town in an effort to keep him away from her not-too-bright teenage daughter, Mamie (Quentin Dean). Joe's stepmother, Annie (Katy Jurado), craves such status symbols as indoor plumbing. He finally gets that for her, but before she is able to use it, the fancy improvements cave in. Joe also almost ruins his sister Mary's marriage with his well-intentioned but catastrophic misdeeds. Joe's father (Burgess Meredith) is plagued by his nagging wife, and his grandfather (Thomas Gomez) has no use for the modern notions and still hasn't put aside the idea of scalping the white man. Joe throws a wild, uninhibited party for his hard-drinking Navajo neighbors, which ends in mayhem, gunshots and a slaughtered bull (mistaken for a cow), which provides the nourishment. Joe then begins selling the cows the government gave him in an attempt to raise money to buy another bull. Finally, after a series of comic episodes, when it appears the family will go to jail for selling government property, Joe saves the day by selling his car piece by piece and winning a bull-riding contest. The day and the film end with a big fight in which Joe's house comes crashing down. From out of the rubble Joe's head appears. He looks around and says, "Sure was one hell of a fight."

with Quentin Dean

with Katy Jurado and Burgess Meredith

Elvis really looking great and playing in a wild knock-'em-down comedy. To please the fans, Elvis manages to sing a couple of songs. *Stay Away, Joe* stands out because it is the only free-for-all comedy Elvis has done and it's so different from what you'd expect that you like it because of its insanity. The film presented a different kind of Presley.

A Metro-Goldwyn-Mayer Picture (1968)

Cast

Elvis Presley, Nancy Sinatra, Bill Bixby, Gale Gordon, William Schallert, Victoria Meyerink, Carl Ballantine, Ross Hagen

Credits

Produced by Douglas Laurence. Directed by Norman Taurog. Written by Philip Shuken.

Synopsis

Steve Grayson (Elvis Presley) has a solid record as a winner, both personally and as a champion auto racer. His wallet is always filled and the ladies love him. Generosity is the keynote to his personality, and when he sees someone in need, he always comes to the rescue. Kenny Donford (Bill Bixby) is Steve's best friend, a charming but rather irresponsible guy who serves as the champ's "business manager." It's Kenny who handles Steve's secret "charities"—such as buying a new station-wagon for a poor family and furniture for newlyweds.

Life is a lark for the pair as they travel from track to track until the Internal Revenue informs Steve that he is almost $100,000 in debt thanks to Kenny's interpretation of tax forms. Steve consults a business management firm which assigns a young employee, Susan Jacks (Nancy Sinatra), to travel with the boys, collecting the winnings and paying Uncle Sam. Gorgeous though she is, there is an instant clash between the high-living driver and the penny-pinching mathematician. The final blow comes when Steve learns that Kenny has lost all the money on horses when it was supposed to help their needy friends.

Steve feels morally responsible for the straits of his friends and obliged to settle his personal debts and pacify his creditors. But, since Susan will only allow him $100 per week for living expenses, their romance cools. Steve resolves to sell his beloved racer, as the only solution, since it will bring ten to fifteen thousand dollars. Just as his archrival, Paul Dado (Ross Hagen), is about to make the purchase, Susan bursts in with the news that the government has granted a temporary reprieve so Steve can settle his personal obligations.

Steve enters the big "Charlotte 600" race, goes on to win it, pays his debts and goes on to win Susan, too.

with Nancy Sinatra

Elvis costarred with the fine-looking Nancy Sinatra, who was riding high on the recording charts at the time. Romance blossoms as Elvis qualifies for the "Charlotte 600" race in a film that includes a discotheque whose booths are cars sawed in half and some fascinating racing shots. The soundtrack recording was only fair. *Speedway* could have been called *Viva Las Vegas–Part 2*.

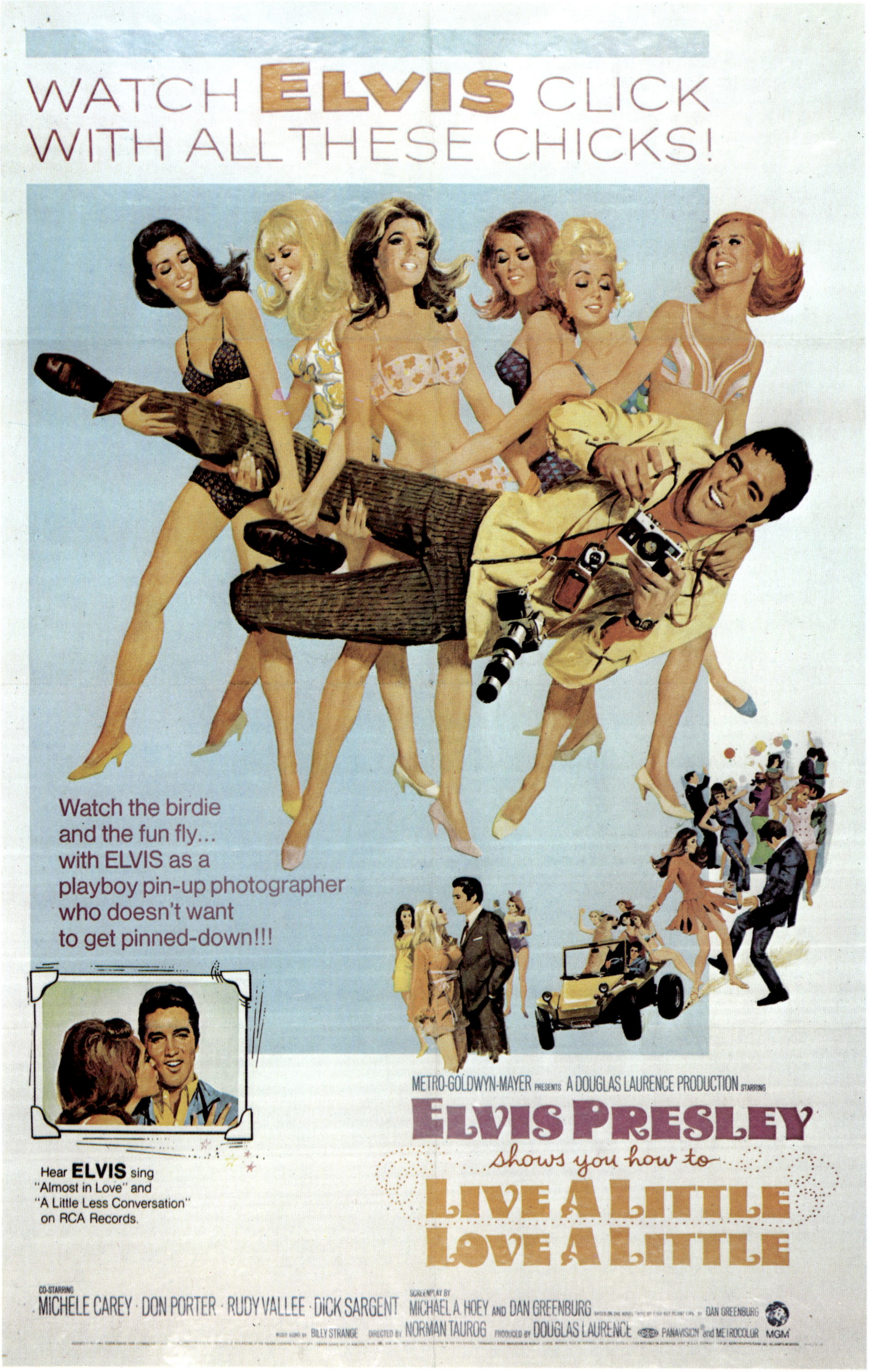
WATCH ELVIS CLICK
WITH ALL THESE CHICKS!
Watch the birdie
and the fun fly...
with ELVIS as a
playboy pin-up photographer
who doesn't want
to get pinned-down!!!
Hear ELVIS sing
"Almost in Love" and
"A Little Less Conversation"
on RCA Records.
METRO-GOLDWYN-MAYER PRESENTS A DOUGLAS LAURENCE PRODUCTION STARRING
ELVIS PRESLEY
shows you how to
LIVE A LITTLE
LOVE A LITTLE
CO-STARRING
MICHELE CAREY · DON PORTER · RUDY VALLEE · DICK SARGENT
SCREENPLAY BY
MICHAEL A. HOEY AND DAN GREENBURG
DAN GREENBURG
BILLY STRANGE
DIRECTED BY NORMAN TAUROG
PRODUCED BY DOUGLAS LAURENCE
PANAVISION® and METROCOLOR
MGM

A Metro-Goldwyn-Mayer Picture (1968)

Cast

Elvis Presley, Michele Carey, Don Porter, Rudy Vallee, Dick Sargent, Sterling Holloway, Celeste Yarnall

Credits

Produced by Douglas Laurence. Directed by Norman Taurog. Screenplay by Michael A. Hoey and Dan Greenburg. Based on the novel *Kiss My Firm but Pliant Lips* by Dan Greenburg.

Synopsis

Greg Nolan (Elvis Presley) is a photographer working for a Los Angeles newspaper. The movie begins with Greg in a dune buggy, singing over the opening credits as he drives down to the beach. Before long, his privacy is interrupted by Bernice (Michele Carey) and her Great Dane, Albert (Albert). While Greg clearly wants to be left alone, Bernice has other ideas. So she has Albert chase Greg into the water and does not let him come out until nightfall. By this time Greg has developed a mild case of pneumonia, and Bernice takes him up to the beach house, gives him some pills and puts him to bed. While recovering, Greg sleeps continuously for several days. When he finally awakens and tries to resume his usual activities, he finds that he has been fired from his job at the newspaper.

After losing his job, the next thing Greg loses is his apartment. Bernice had gone over and moved him out while he was at the beach house. As a result, he is forced to move in with Bernice for a few days (separate rooms, of course). During his stay, Greg has a nightmare which leads into a dream sequence production number titled "Edge of Reality."

Along with her other problems, including her ex-boyfriend, Harry (Dick Sargent), who keeps hanging around, Bernice has a penchant for changing her name throughout the movie, much to Greg's dismay. The dream song deals with Greg's confusion over this and his entire relationship with Bernice (and Albert). Greg then goes out and finds two jobs as a commercial photographer for two opposing firms located in the same building. One of his bosses, Mike Lansdown (Don Porter), is very liberal and informal, while the other, Penlow (Rudy Vallee), is very strict and conservative, thus causing Greg to constantly adjust his appearance, habits and personality.

To celebrate his new jobs, Bernice goes out and finds Greg a beautiful new house and comes over with Harry to have dinner. As Harry and Greg have never gotten along very well, the dinner ends quickly and Bernice leaves with Harry. A few days later, Bernice returns to tell Greg that she has decided to leave Harry and the beach house for good. So now, Bernice has nowhere to go and is forced to move in with Greg. As there is only one bedroom, Greg places a board between the two of them in bed. However, after exercising more physical restraint than any man and woman could ever bear, Greg and Bernice finally get together.

At this point, Bernice is so confused as to what she wants, she runs away. Not to be discouraged, Greg follows her, finds her at the beach, pours out his undying love and devotion, and Greg, Bernice and Albert all live happily ever after. At the conclusion, Greg has Albert chase Bernice into the water and then goes in after her for a wild, romantic, comic, splashing, kissing finale.

with Michele Carey

An odd cross of comedy and subdued effects, with Elvis having a dream brought on by a pill given to him by the extremely beautiful Michele Carey. Together with this very sexy lady, Elvis and his honest approach carried this film over its rough spots. Elvis' personality was delightful, and this, along with his great gift of humor, made this one of his most pleasurable movies.

SOMETHING DIFFERENT

During this period, Elvis made three films—the excellent *Charro!*, the above-average *Change of Habit* and the fair *Trouble with Girls.* Unfortunately, the movie houses were either booking Elvis pictures as the second feature or not showing them at all. The "lazy years" had certainly had their effect.

National General Pictures offered Elvis something different—a dramatic role and a departure from the pap he'd been making for the last six or seven years. In *Charro!* he appeared unshaven and disheveled. To say the bearded Elvis looked incredible would be an understatement. He added a new dimension to his screen career in this film. But it did little at the box-office.

Presley movies had always been a combination of laughs, love and songs—until Universal starred Elvis in *Change of Habit.* The studio had offered Elvis a chance to do something different and he was quick to take it. The contemporary story of *Change of Habit* revolved around modern problems and social issues, with Elvis playing a doctor and Mary Tyler Moore playing a modern nun. The film explored the same problems and questions that make newspaper headlines—offering Elvis a dramatic role.

Elvis' next was for MGM. In *The Trouble With Girls* Elvis did not appear for most of the first forty-five minutes. Although he looked great when he did appear, the story was weak and the film was not shown in most of the major cities.

Despite the repeated warning that the cannon will destroy the town, Jess refuses to release Billy Roy. A shot topples the heavy church bell; another kills the sheriff and destroys his house. The townspeople urge Jess to free Billy Roy, and Jess rides out of town with him. The people aren't sure if he has left for their sake or defected.

The pair approach Vince's gang and Jess demands they surrender. If they shoot, he tells them, he will kill Billy Roy. A fight ensues and several members of the gang are killed. Billy Roy dies when the wagon with the cannon breaks loose and crushes him.

The fight is over and Vince is a beaten man. Jess takes him prisoner and drives the wagon back into town. When the townspeople see what he has done, they ask Jess to remain with them as sheriff. Jess declines, saying that he must return the cannon and Vince to Mexico.

Tracy asks if he will be coming back. Jess says no, but he promises to send for her. He slowly rides out of town.

with Ina Balin

with Ina Balin

The ads read "A different kind of man . . . a different kind of role." And indeed it was. We have a dirty, bearded Elvis in this one. Elvis looks simply handsome and turns in a performance that deserves some kind of award. A very rough, Clint Eastwood-type western. If you are not a western fan, certainly Elvis' performance alone is worth the price of admission.

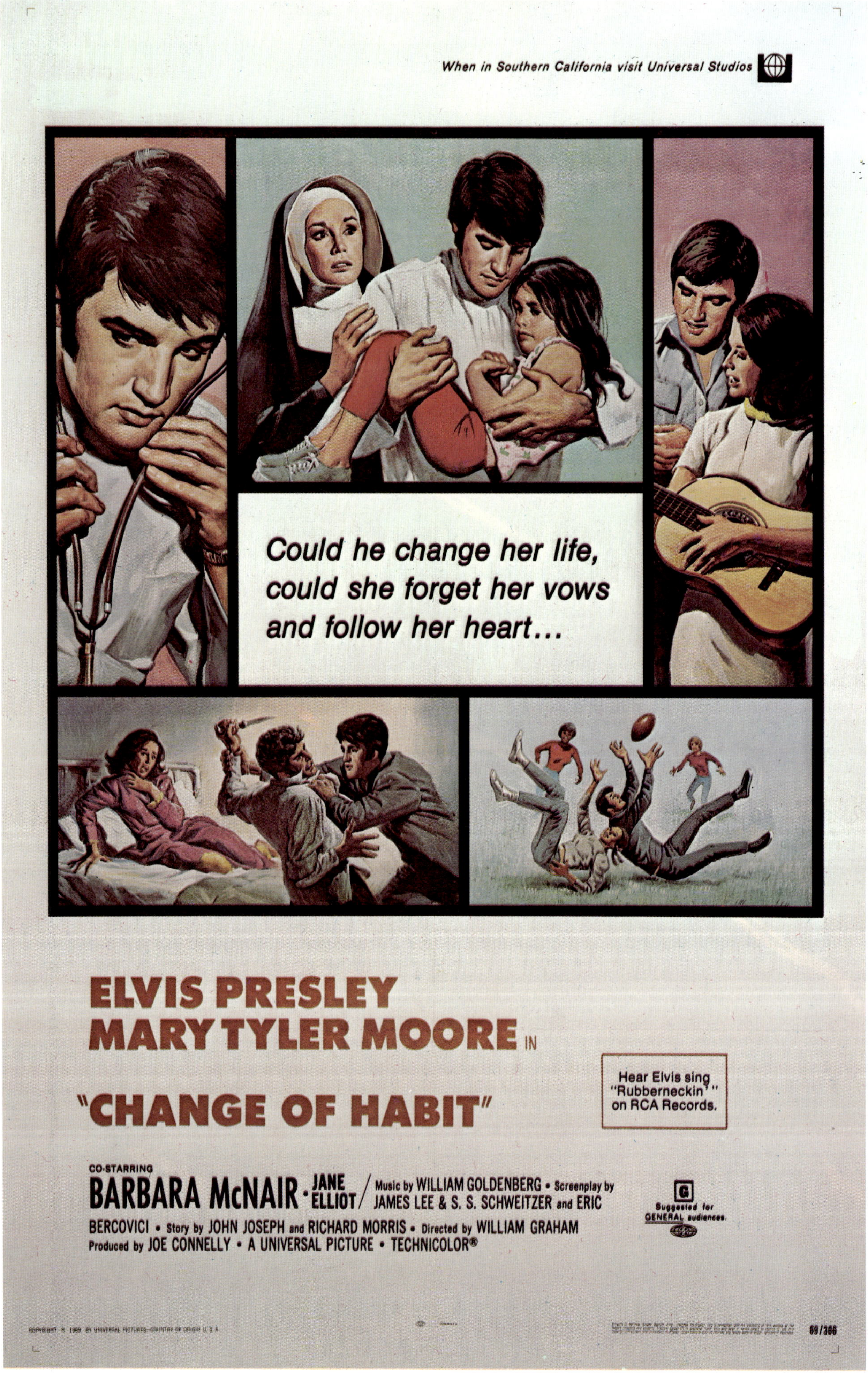
When in Southern California visit Universal Studios
Could he change her life, could she forget her vows and follow her heart...
ELVIS PRESLEY
MARY TYLER MOORE IN
"CHANGE OF HABIT"
Hear Elvis sing "Rubberneckin'" on RCA Records.
CO-STARRING
BARBARA McNAIR · JANE ELLIOT / Music by WILLIAM GOLDENBERG • Screenplay by JAMES LEE & S. S. SCHWEITZER and ERIC BERCOVICI • Story by JOHN JOSEPH and RICHARD MORRIS • Directed by WILLIAM GRAHAM
Produced by JOE CONNELLY • A UNIVERSAL PICTURE • TECHNICOLOR®
G Suggested for GENERAL audiences.
COPYRIGHT © 1969 BY UNIVERSAL PICTURES—COUNTRY OF ORIGIN U. S. A.
69/366

A Universal Picture (1969)

Cast

Elvis Presley, Mary Tyler Moore, Barbara McNair,
Jane Elliot, Leora Dana, Edward Asner, Robert Emhardt, Regis Toomey

Credits

Produced by Joe Connelly. Directed by William Graham.
Screenplay by James Lee & S. S. Schweitzer and Eric Bercovici.
Story by John Joseph and Richard Morris.

Synopsis

Dr. John Carpenter (Elvis Presley) comes into contact with three nuns, Sister Michelle (Mary Tyler Moore), Sister Irene (Barbara McNair) and Sister Barbara (Jane Elliot) when they arrive in his ghetto area in plain clothes. The sisters are to get practical experience in the real world before taking their final vows. To this end, they take an apartment every bit as dingy and depressing as those of their neighbors.

Although they are attached to the local clergyman, Father Gibbons (Regis Toomey), he dislikes their presence intensely and frowns on their dress, ideas of recreation, manners and everything else about the three novices.

Dr. Carpenter finds himself very attracted to Sister Michelle and is very puzzled at her avoidance of his attentions. The other nuns also run into unusual problems in the outside world, regarding race relations and social behavior. They manage to cope with their problems, however—all except Sister Michelle, who endeavors to teach a young girl to speak with the help of the doctor.

After a big block party, which makes the three nuns feel even more a part of the outside world, they are ordered by the Mother Superior (Leora Dana) to return to the convent. Sisters Michelle and Irene choose to return; Sister Barbara does not. In his surgery, Dr. Carpenter asks Michelle to explain why she has never returned his affection. When she tells him the truth, he angrily asks her if she has taken the vow of honesty. He is anguished because she has allowed him to fall in love with her in the first place.

As Dr. Carpenter sings "Let's Pray Together" at a folk mass in the ghetto church, Sister Michelle enters the church and we are left to ponder whether she has come back for good or just to see the man she obviously has a strong feeling for.

with Mary Tyler Moore

This film really was a change of habit—with Elvis really acting. The mobs of pretty girls were gone and, in their place, we had a contemporary film. Elvis looked better than ever before. He sang only a few very good tunes. If Elvis were to continue to make quality films such as this one, he could easily become recognized as a fine actor.

A Metro-Goldwyn-Mayer Picture (1969)

Cast

Elvis Presley, Marlyn Mason, Vincent Price, John Carradine, Sheree North, Joyce Van Patten, Edward Andrews, Bill Zuckert, Dabney Coleman, Anthony Teague

Credits

Produced by Lester Welch. Directed by Peter Tewksbury. Screenplay by Arnold and Lois Peyser. From the novel by Day Keene and Dwight Babcock.

Synopsis

It's the roaring 20's. To the blaring music of a marching band, the Chautauqua roars into Radford Center. The excitement and enthusiasm of the people of Radford Center are reflected by the new manager of the traveling show, Walter Hale (Elvis Presley), who grew up in the business, first as a singer and then as a manager. Beyond his managerial responsibilities, Hale has a special problem in the person of Charlene (Marlyn Mason), a constant fighter for union rights among the Chautauqua performers. She and Hale are in constant battle for this reason, but between them a mutual admiration is growing.

In spite of the general atmosphere of gaiety, there is a somber note reflected by Harrison Wilby (Dabney Coleman), the town druggist, who is carrying on with Nita Bix (Sheree North). All the high spirits disappear when Wilby's body is found floating in the town lake. A member of the show, Clarence (Anthony Teague), is arrested for murder in spite of his protestations of innocence. It remains for Hale to determine the identity of the real killer, but, when he turns this knowledge to financial advantage for the Chautauqua company, he incurs the wrath of Charlene.

But Hale puts on a slam-bang final show, even to the public unmasking of the murderer, and by the time the final curtain falls, all but his romantic problem has been resolved.

This particular problem takes a little longer.

with Marlyn Mason

Elvis hardly appears in the first forty minutes of the film. He looks sensational. *The Trouble with Girls* contains no standout songs and an absolutely insane title that has nothing at all to do with the film. The story line was very simple and not very good. All in all, just not a very memorable film.

THE IMAGE

It was announced that Elvis' thirty-second film, MGM's *Elvis—That's the Way It is,* would be something different and special. It was. The film was a semidocumentary, capturing Elvis' rehearsals as well as his record-breaking show at the International Hotel in Las Vegas. But, while the show was the core of the film, the film went beyond that, showing Elvis preparing the show, sweating, caring and worrying like any other human being.

Elvis never looked better, and to say that his show was perhaps the greatest ever given by any human would be an understatement. The only fault I could find with this excellent film would be the Colonel's choice of fans that were spotlighted during the film. To say they represented the average Elvis fan would be embarrassing.

Elvis finally shared part of his private life in his thirty-third film, MGM's *Elvis on Tour.* With a national concert tour as a musical and visual backdrop, much of Presley's life crosses the screen, punctuated by the star's own recollections of how it all happened. The rest is history.

The RCA Records fact sheet indicates twenty-six million-selling albums and over one hundred million single-record sales. Today his following is broader than it's ever been. In January of 1973, Elvis' "Aloha from Hawaii" TV show was beamed via satellite and was seen by more people than man's first walk on the moon.

It is this writer's hope that Elvis will one day make that one great film that he's capable of. His film career is one of the last great ones in Hollywood, and he himself is a great actor—a natural.

A Metro-Goldwyn-Mayer Picture (1970)

Credits

Directed by Denis Sanders. Director of Photography—Lucien Ballard. Edited by Henry Berman, A.C.E. Production Manager—Dale Hutchinson. Assistant Director—John Wilson. Associate Film Editor—George Folsey, Jr. Technical Advisor—Colonel Tom Parker.

Contents

For his thirty-second motion picture, Elvis Presley portrayed himself as the artist and the phenomenon he is. Academy Award-winning director Denis Sanders explains, "The subject of this film is Elvis, and the core is Elvis on stage in Las Vegas performing his incredible, record-breaking act."

Sanders continues, "However, we went much further with the cameras. We attempted to capture the ups and downs he experiences putting his show together, showing the man as a musician. We filmed both sides of the lights, exploring what he feels and the emotions he creates in others."

Pursuing that goal, the director photographed his subject in private rehearsals at MGM studios, further rehearsals in Las Vegas and then onstage in the Showroom Internationale of the International Hotel. Cameras were also there on September 9, in Phoenix, Arizona, for the opening of the star's first concert tour in thirteen years. To gain insight into Elvis' following, Sanders interviewed businessmen, students housewives and others, talking with a variety of people who have literally devoted varying portions of their existences to the former teenage truck driver named Elvis Presley. Sanders also traveled to Luxembourg to capture the Fifth Annual Elvis Presley Appreciation Society Convention.

Of Elvis, the Mississippi-born, Tennessee-raised overnight sensation, who literally changed the course of popular music, little remains to be said. Judged by almost any standard, the RCA Victor Records artist is the most singularly successful entertainer in history.

After all of his gold records—and his golden records at the box-offices of theaters around the world—*That's the Way It Is* finally managed to tell his admirers a little more about the man who has intrigued them than they ever knew before.

For more than fifteen years, Elvis Presley's fans have referred to him as "The King." In this film, he finally emerges from the trappings of plot and song-and-dance routines to prove just how securely he still wears that crown. *That's the Way It Is* aims at being entertainment, but along the way it becomes a window where we can view his realm.

with Sammy Davis, Jr.

Elvis' thirty-second movie stands out as a monument to him and his music. Elvis has never looked as handsome as in this 1969 documentary. I'm pleased to say that this is not only one of his best, it is one of the best of all time. The soundtrack LP is excellent. The King is in complete command of the film.

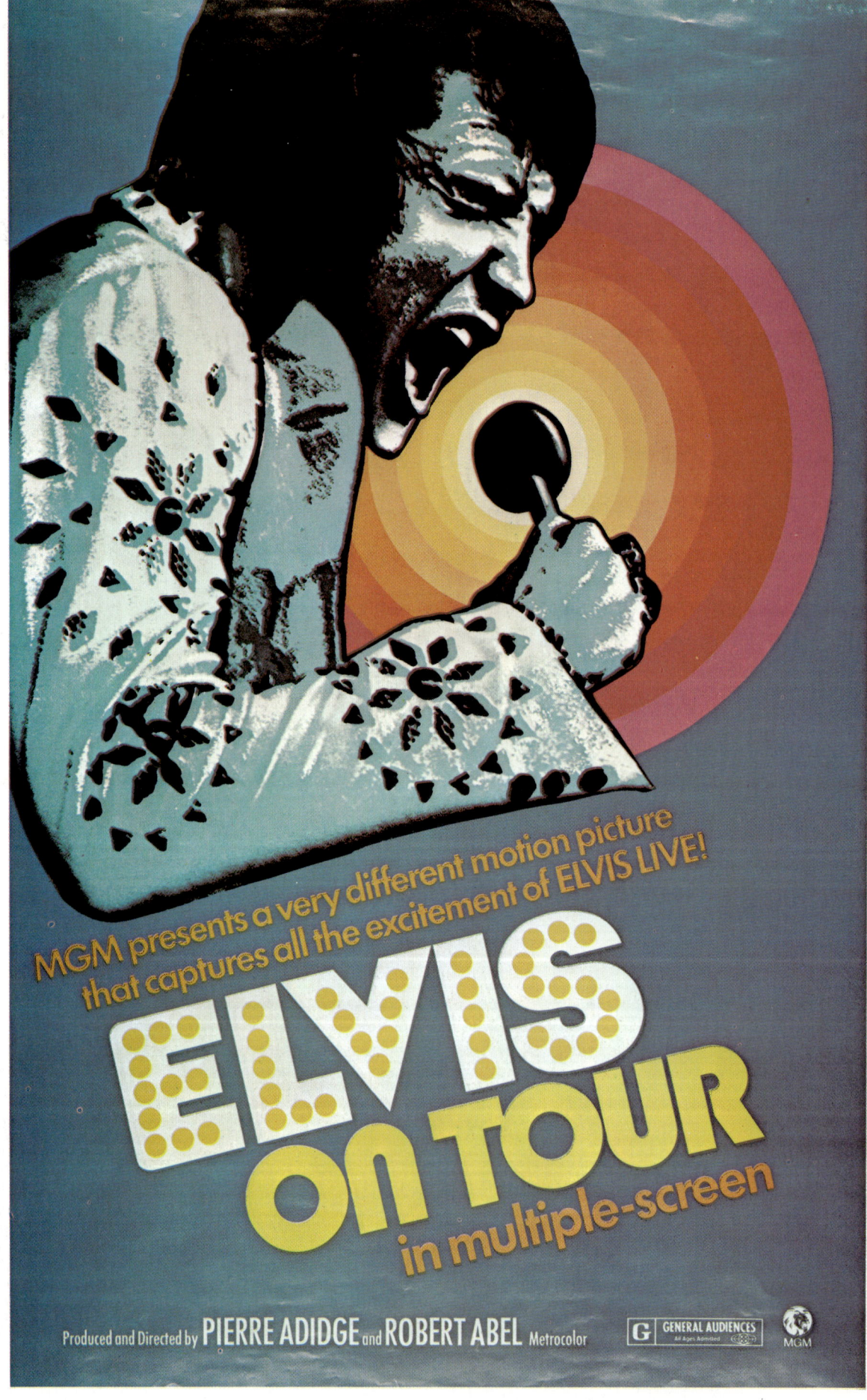

A Metro-Goldwyn-Mayer Picture (1972)

Credits

Produced and Directed by Pierre Adidge and Robert Abel.
Technical Advisor—Colonel Tom Parker.
Associate Producer—Sidney Levin. Edited by Ken Zemke.
Director of Photography—Robert E. Thomas.

Contents

"My daddy had seen a lot of people who played guitars and stuff and didn't work, so he said, 'You should make up your mind either about being an electrician or playing a guitar. I never saw a guitar player that was worth a damn.'"

These words, spoken by Elvis Presley, open *Elvis on Tour*. In this film, for the first time in his career, the legendary entertainer reveals a part of himself and his past. Elvis Presley—the American phenomenon—set to the sights and sounds of his record-breaking concert tours.

"Elvis was guarded at first," according to producers–directors Pierre Adidge and Robert Abel. "He's a very private and, in some ways, shy person. But, after we filmed him on tour and were allowed to shoot and record in places he had never allowed cameras in the past, we finally asked if he would mind talking about himself. He thought awhile and finally agreed.

"We don't like to pose people and we don't like to ask questions. So we collected a number of photographs from his past and simply recorded his reactions. Ultimately, he forgot about the recorder, and we had two good sessions which not only make the film complete but set the record straight on several matters."

Elvis' voice is heard over film of his concerts, combined with never-before-seen pictures chosen from his family album. Also included is footage from his early career, such as his first appearance on the Ed Sullivan show. He discusses his reaction to the impact of his first public appearance and, much earlier, the first time he remembers singing. He reminisces about being entered in a talent show when he was eight years old and another contest when he was in the eleventh grade.

"I came on stage (and) heard people kind of rumbling and whispering and so forth 'cause nobody knew I even sang," Elvis says. "It was amazing how popular I became in school after that." He concludes a discussion of the days prior to stardom with, "I made that first record really as a personal thing for my mother. And that same company called me a year later and said, 'We got a song you might be able to do.' It was 12 o'clock and they said, 'Can you be here by 3 o'clock?' I was there by the time they hung up the phone!"

Now, almost one hundred million single records and approximately twenty-six million-selling albums later, *Elvis on Tour* marks his thirty-third motion picture. At last, his daddy knows a guitar player "worth a damn."

On Tour is Elvis' last film to date and, again, a documentary. And what a great film it is. Typically, the Motion Picture Academy failed to even nominate it in the documentary category, although the film won the Golden Globe Award as best documentary of the year. The photography was unique and we saw as many as twelve Elvises on screen at the same time. The tragic thing about leaving Elvis out of even a nominating category is that politics mean more than effort. If Elvis was everybody's buddy in the industry, he would have been nominated. To top that off, certainly one of the songs in the film should have qualified for an Academy nomination.

MOVIE MUSIC

ALBUM

LOVE ME TENDER
RCA 45 EP (OP)*
Love Me Tender; Let Me; Poor Boy; We're Gonna Move
Note—Final verse of "Love Me Tender" is unavailable on RCA.

LOVING YOU
RCA 33⅓ LP
Got a Lot o' Livin' to Do; Blueberry Hill; Mean Woman Blues; (Let Me Be Your) Teddy Bear; Loving You; Lonesome Cowboy; Hot Dog; Party; True Love; Don't Leave Me Now; Have I Told You Lately That I Love You?; I Need You So
Note—Songs not included in film or record: "Candy Kisses," "Dancing on a Dare," "We're Gonna Live It Up." While RCA lists this as an original soundtrack LP, all songs differ from the movie.

JAILHOUSE ROCK
RCA 45 EP (OP)
Jailhouse Rock; Young and Beautiful; I Want to Be Free; Don't Leave Me Now; (You're so Square) Baby, I Don't Care (out of print)
Note—Movie versions of "Jailhouse Rock," "Treat Me Nice" differ from those on record.

KING CREOLE
RCA 33⅓ LP
Trouble; Crawfish; King Creole; As Long As I Have You; Hard Headed Woman; Dixieland Rock; Young Dreams; Steadfast, Loyal and True; New Orleans
Note—Song not included in film or record: "Danny."

G.I. BLUES
RCA 33⅓ LP
Tonight Is So Right for Love; What's She Really Like?; Frankfort Special; Wooden Heart; G.I. Blues; Pocketful of Rainbows; Shoppin' Around; Big Boots; Didja' Ever; Blue Suede Shoes; Doin' the Best I Can
Note—Different version called "Tonight's All Right for Love" (on LP *Legendary Performer*).

FLAMING STAR
RCA 33⅓ EP (OP)
Both "Flaming Star" and "Summer Kisses, Winter Tears" were available on RCA 33⅓ EP *Elvis by Request*.
Note—"A Cane and a High Starched Collar" in film, but not available on record. "Britches" cut out of film, not available on record; "Summer Kisses, Winter Tears" cut out of film, available on record.

WILD IN THE COUNTRY
RCA 45 (OP)
Title song was released as RCA 45 single.
Note—"Husky Dusky Day"—available on RCA records.
"Lonely Man" (seen in trailer), "Forget Me Never."

BLUE HAWAII
RCA 33⅓ LP
Blue Hawaii; Almost Always True; Aloha-Oe; No More; Can't Help Falling in Love; Rock-A-Hula Baby; Moonlight Swim; Ku-U-I-Po (Hawaiian Sweetheart); Ito Eats; Slicin' Sand; Hawaiian Sunset; Beach Boy Blues; Island of Love; Hawaiian Wedding Song
Note—"Steppin' Out of Line," "La Paloma," "Playing with Fire" were cut from film and are not available.

FOLLOW THAT DREAM
RCA 45 EP (OP)
Follow That Dream; Angel; What a Wonderful Life; I'm Not the Marrying Kind (out of print)
Note—"Sound Advice" (available on RCA LP *Elvis for Everyone*).
"On Top of Old Smokey" heard in film—not available on record.

KID GALAHAD
RCA 45 EP (OP)
King of the Whole Wide World; This Is Living; Riding the Rainbow; Home Is Where the Heart Is; I Got Lucky; A Whistling Tune
Note—"Love Is For Lovers" (cut from film—not available on RCA).

GIRLS! GIRLS! GIRLS!
RCA 33⅓ LP
Girls! Girls! Girls!; I Don't Wanna Be Tied; Where Do You Come From?; I Don't Want To; We'll Be Together; A Boy Like Me, a Girl Like You; Earth Boy; Return to Sender; Because of Love; Thanks to the Rolling Sea; Song of the Shrimp; The Walls Have Ears; We're Coming in Loaded
Note—"Plantation Rock," "Twist Me Loose," "Pot Pourri" (cut from film—not available on RCA).

*EP stands for "extended play" (45 or 33⅓ RPM), in the same size as a single. EP's came in small cardboard covers and contained four to six songs. OP indicates "out of print."

IT HAPPENED AT THE WORLD'S FAIR RCA 33⅓ LP (OP)	Beyond the Bend; Relax; Take Me to the Fair; They Remind Me Too Much of You; One Broken Heart for Sale; I'm Falling in Love Tonight; Cotton Candy Land; A World of Our Own; How Would You Like to Be; Happy Ending
FUN IN ACAPULCO RCA 33⅓ LP	Fun in Acapulco; El Toro; Marguerita; The Bullfighter Was a Lady; I Think I'm Gonna Like It Here; Bossa Nova Baby; Guadalajara; Vino, Dinero y Amor; You Can't Say No in Acapulco; Love Me Tonight; Slowly but Surely; (There's) No Room to Rhumba in a Sports Car; Mexico
KISSIN' COUSINS RCA 33⅓ LP	Kissin' Cousins; Barefoot Ballad; Catchin' on Fast; Once Is Enough; One Boy, Two Little Girls; Smokey Mountain Boy; Tender Feeling; There's Gold in the Mountains; Anyone (Could Fall in Love with You); Kissin' Cousins (number 2); Echoes of Love; (It's a) Long Lonely Highway. Note—"Anyone (Could Fall In Love With You)" was cut out of the film, but the song is available on RCA.
VIVA LAS VEGAS RCA 45 EP (OP)	If You Think I Don't Need You; I Need Somebody to Lean On; C'mon Everybody; Today, Tomorrow and Forever Note—"Do the Vega" (cut from film—not available on RCA). "You're the Boss," "The Lady Loves Me" are in film, but not available on RCA.
ROUSTABOUT RCA 33⅓ LP	Roustabout; Little Egypt; Poison Ivy League; Hard Knocks; It's a Wonderful World; Big Love Big Heartache; One Track Heart; It's Carnival Time; Carny Town; There's a Brand New Day on the Horizon; Wheels on My Heels
GIRL HAPPY RCA 33⅓ LP	Girl Happy; Spring Fever; Fort Lauderdale Chamber of Commerce; Startin'; Tonight; Cross My Heart and Hope to Die; The Meanest Girl in Town; Puppet on a String; I've Got to Find My Baby; You'll Be Gone; Wolf Call; Do Not Disturb; Do the Clam
TICKLE ME RCA 45 EP (OP)	I Feel That I've Known You Forever; Slowly but Surely; Nightrider; Put the Blame on Me; Dirty, Dirty Feeling Note—All songs in this film were taken from earlier Elvis LP's. The RCA EP featured only five of the nine songs from the film.
HARUM SCARUM RCA 33⅓ LP (OP)	Harem Holiday; Golden Coins; Hey Little Girl; My Desert Serenade; Kismet; Go East Young Man; So Close, Yet So Far; Mirage; Shake That Tambourine; Animal Instinct; Wisdom of the Ages Note—"Animal Instinct," "Wisdom of the Ages" (cut from film, but available on RCA).
PARADISE, HAWAIIAN STYLE RCA 33⅓ LP	Paradise, Hawaiian Style; This Is My Heaven; Scratch My Back; House of Sand; A Dog's Life; Queenie Wahine's Papaya; Drums of the Islands; Stop Where You Are; Sand Castles
FRANKIE AND JOHNNY RCA 33⅓ LP (OP)	Frankie and Johnny; Come Along; Petunia, the Gardener's Daughter; Chesay; What Every Woman Lives For; Look Out, Broadway; Beginner's Luck; Down by the Riverside and When the Saints Go Marching In; Shout It Out; Hard Luck; Please Don't Stop Loving Me; Everybody Come Aboard
SPINOUT RCA 33⅓ LP (OP)	Spinout; Stop, Look and Listen; Adam and Evil; All That I Am; Never Say Yes; Am I Ready; Beach Shack; Smorgasbord; I'll Be Back; Tomorrow Is a Long Time; Down in the Alley; I'll Remember You

EASY COME, EASY GO RCA 45 EP	Easy Come, Easy Go; Love Machine; Yoga Is As Yoga Does; You Gotta Stop; Sing, You Children; I'll Take Love
DOUBLE TROUBLE RCA 33⅓ LP (OP)	Old MacDonald; Double Trouble; Baby, If You'll Give Me All of Your Love; Could I Fall in Love; Long Legged Girl (with the Short Dress On); City by Night; I Love Only One Girl; There is So Much World to See; It Won't Be Long; Never Ending; Blue River; What Now, What Next, Where To? (out of print)
CLAMBAKE RCA 33⅓ LP (OP)	Clambake; Who Needs Money?; A House That Has Everything; Confidence; Hey, Hey, Hey; The Girl I Never Loved; You Don't Know Me; Guitar Man; How Can You Lose What You Never Had?; Big Boss Man; Singing Tree; Just Call Me Lonesome (out of print)
STAY AWAY, JOE RCA 45 RPM (OP)	Note—"Goin' Home" cut from film. "Dominique" heard in film, not on RCA.
SPEEDWAY RCA 33⅓ LP	Speedway; There Ain't Nothing Like a Song (with Nancy Sinatra); Your Time Hasn't Come Yet, Baby; Who Are You?; He's Your Uncle, Not Your Dad; Let Yourself Go; Your Groovy Self (with Nancy Sinatra). Bonus Songs: Five Sleepy Heads; Western Union; Mine; Goin' Home; Suppose. Note—"Five Sleepy Heads," "Suppose," "Western Union" cut from film, available on RCA.
LIVE A LITTLE, LOVE A LITTLE RCA 45 (OP)	A Little Less Conversation; Almost in Love available on RCA 45 RPM. Let's Live A Little (cut from film, not on RCA)
CHARRO RCA 45 (OP)	Charro
THE TROUBLE WITH GIRLS	Note—"Signs of the Zodiac" heard in film, not available on RCA.
CHANGE OF HABIT	Note—"Rubberneckin' " released on RCA 45 RPM; "Change of Habit," "Let Us Pray," "Have a Happy" are available on various Elvis budget LP's.
ELVIS: THAT'S THE WAY IT IS RCA 33⅓ LP	I Just Can't Help Believin'; Twenty Days and Twenty Nights; How the Web Was Woven; Patch It Up; Mary in the Morning; You Don't Have to Say You Love Me; You've Lost That Lovin' Feeling; I've Lost You; Just Pretend; Stranger in the Crowd; The Next Step Is Love; Bridge over Troubled Water Note—Only "I Just Can't Help Believin' " is from the film soundtrack; all the others are studio cuts.
ELVIS ON TOUR	Separate Ways; That's All Right Mama; Memories; Mystery Train. The other songs in the film are not available on RCA. However, other versions of same songs are. Note—"Sweet Sweet Spirit," "The Lighthouse," "Rainy Night in Georgia" not on RCA.

All of the above records, including the out-of-print records, are available through:

ELVIS UNIQUE RECORD CLUB
P. O. BOX 339
HUNTINGDON VALLEY, PA 19006

ABOUT THE AUTHOR

Paul Lichter is as unique as his record club—the Elvis Unique Record Club. He is a man in quest of Elvis, and it certainly looks as if he has found his way. He dresses and styles his hair in the Presley fashion. At first glance, one would tend to believe that he is trying to be the King himself, but after getting to know him, you find that he is just showing his appreciation for Elvis' taste in style. He carries that style quite well.

Born on September 24, 1944 (for you astrology buffs, that makes him a Libra on the cusp of Virgo), his first introduction to Elvis was a gift from his parents—two records. "That's All Right, Mama"/"Blue Moon of Kentucky" and "Good Rockin' Tonight"/"I Don't Care If the Sun Don't Shine" in 1954. At the tender age of ten, Paul was on his way. After viewing Elvis on the tube (Dorsey Show), he knew he was hooked on the Presley fever. Being too young to do anything about it, he was content with just buying the records and paying his quarter to get into the Saturday matinee and watch his movies.

In 1970 a change came about for this man (and lucky for us it did). This year brought about a whole new slant in the life of Paul and Janice Lichter, his lovely wife. Blessed with two fine children, a boy, Kyle, age 9, and a girl, Danielle, or Dan Dan, age 6, and their miniature collie named (what else?) Elvis, Paul was ready to do something about the driving urge inside him. It marked the beginning of the Elvis Unique Record Club—started mainly because there wasn't enough good Elvis material available to the real Elvis fans. This club boasts more Elvis memorabilia than Elvis himself has.

Paul has met Elvis on numerous occasions, the first of which occurred in 1971 in Las Vegas. He says that this is his most treasured experience. For a limited amount of time he was one of the few people who have been admitted into the guarded Presley circle. His opinion of Elvis is high. "Elvis is very kind, a hell of a nice guy. Anyone lucky enough to know him would be proud to be his fan." His most treasured possession is the red "Burning Love" jumpsuit, which he obtained in Nashville, Tennessee, in March of 1974 during the Cerebral Palsy Telethon in which he donated an original Sun record and $5,000 in the name of the *Memphis Flash*. He also answered phones for pledges.

Paul has every record Elvis ever recorded in 78's, 45's and 33 1/3's, plus films of the King in action, books and magazines that would boggle the mind of the most avid Presley freak. All of these are available through his record club (PO Box 339, Huntingdon Valley, Pennsylvania 19006).

The *Memphis Flash* originated in January of 1974, and already it boasts 16,000 nation- and worldwide members. It is one of the best, if not the best "fanzine" printed on the King, chock-full of interesting stories and many little-known facts pertaining to Elvis. It is a must in any Elvis collection.

Paul says that his ultimate goal would be to be considered one of Elvis' close friends. He has met Elvis many times and witnessed more than 600 performances by the King. One can only believe that Paul may somehow reach his goal. Surely this man's work shall not go unrewarded.

His ultimate goal for Elvis is twofold. First of all, he would like to see Elvis do a first-rate movie —something along the lines of *The Sting* or *The Godfather*—with other major stars in costarring roles. Elvis is truly a fine actor, and given the right role he can prove this to the many nonbelievers who have criticized his abilities in the past. Secondly, Paul would like to see him record some songs written by people like Cat Stevens, Paul McCartney or Roy Wood, or perhaps revert to the old days and produce an album entitled *Elvis Sings Elvis*. For rock-a-billy has never really died, and it would take someone, the one who started it all, to revive it again.